T0402588

NORDIC HANDS

25 Fiber Craft Projects to Discover Scandinavian Culture

ANITA OSTERHAUG

SCHIFFER
CRAFT
4880 Lower Valley Road • Atglen, PA 19310

OTHER SCHIFFER CRAFT BOOKS ON RELATED SUBJECTS:

Summer Knitting for Little Sweethearts: 40 Nordic-Style Warm Weather Patterns for Girls, Boys, and Babies,
Hanne Andreassen Hjelmås & Torunn Steinsland, Creators of KlompeLompe, ISBN 978-0-7643-6606-2

Easy Weaving with Supplemental Warps: Overshot, Velvet, Shibori, and More, Deb Essen, ISBN 978-0-7643-6470-9

Norwegian Pick-Up Bandweaving, Heather Torgenrud, ISBN 978-0-7643-4751-1

Cover and interior design by Ashley Millhouse
Photography by Jason Langheine unless otherwise credited
Type set in Starlight/Baskerville

ISBN: 978-0-7643-6691-8
Printed in China

Published by Schiffer Craft
An imprint of Schiffer Publishing, Ltd.
4880 Lower Valley Road
Atglen, PA 19310
Phone: (610) 593-1777; Fax: (610) 593-2002
Email: Info@schifferbooks.com
Web: www.schifferbooks.com

For our complete selection of fine books on this and related subjects, please visit our website at www.schifferbooks.com. You may also write for a free catalog.

Schiffer Publishing's titles are available at special discounts for bulk purchases for sales promotions or premiums. Special editions, including personalized covers, corporate imprints, and excerpts, can be created in large quantities for special needs. For more information, contact the publisher.

We are always looking for people to write books on new and related subjects. If you have an idea for a book, please contact us at proposals@schifferbooks.com.

To my teachers Madelyn van der Hoogt and Syvilla Bolson; to my beloved Aunt Katie, who taught me the joy of Nordic hands; and to my friend Linda Ligon, who taught me that with yarn, words, and curiosity, you can make a very interesting life.

78

110

156

CONTENTS

68

138

128

PREFACE

I grew up surrounded by handmade Nordic textiles, from my family's Norwegian sweaters to the woven runners and blankets that Grandma Osterhaug brought with her from "the old country." I loved them, but as I first learned to knit and craft, there was little information available on traditional Nordic fiber arts. Hand knitting was in a decidedly "mod" stage at that time: "Nordic-inspired" patterns were designed in garish colors, often written to use acrylic yarns that no self-respecting Scandinavian would have touched. And information on Nordic weaving and other fiber arts was mostly unavailable to the average American crafter.

But, thanks to Grandma and my Aunt Katy, plus a local yarn shop that served the heavily Scandinavian Seattle market, I learned Nordic knitting and embroidery techniques. Handwork time was family time, and, to me, that Scandinavian aesthetic was the essence of home. We even made a few *rya* rugs and pillows from imported kits, with Aunt Katy, my mother, and I taking turns working a few rows of knots each day.

Fast-forward twenty years: I had children of my own, Nordic knitting was still a passion, and I had added hand spinning to my craft repertoire. Then Interweave Press announced a fiber arts tour to Scandinavia, the trip of my dreams but outside the budget of my young family. That is, until a friend pointed out that I had a little money left to me by dear Katy, and the best way to honor her legacy would be to go on the trip. It was an adventure that would change the course of my life.

In museums, homes, folk schools, and studios throughout Scandinavia, I fell in love with more kinds of Nordic textiles than I had ever imagined. The Bohus knitting of Sweden, prized by global fashionistas in the mid-twentieth century. Traditional rosepath and *krokbragd* coverlets in warm, harmonious natural colors. Bright, modern rya designs and luxurious handwoven bath towels in Finland. Sunlight streaming through handwoven curtains in a kitchen at Sätergläntan, the Swedish handicraft school. Two-hundred-year-old *båtrye* (boat rya) blankets, wool still heavy with lanolin, made to keep fishermen warm on the North Sea.

And finally, there was a magical midsummer evening at my cousins' cabin at Son, near the entrance to the inner Oslofjord. There on the old pine walls was a hanging made by my great-aunt Elida in Trondheim, with bright-colored wool in a *rutevev* (square weave) design. In that moment, I was hooked for life. I had to learn more about Nordic textiles and how to make them.

In the years since, I've learned to weave Nordic fabrics, from rugs to lace. I've learned band weaving and felting and deepened my knowledge of Nordic knitting. (I also learned that Aunt Elida's hanging actually used an embroidery technique known as *klostersom*.) Along the way, I learned so much more about the culture I grew up with. It wasn't easy at first to find resources. I learned thanks to classes and conferences at the National Nordic Museum in Seattle and at Vesterheim Norwegian-American Museum in Decorah, Iowa; thanks to the Norwegian Textile Guild; and thanks to the amazing teachers—some of whom contributed to this book—and publishers working to keep these crafts alive.

In honor of them, I present this book to you, my fellow crafters who are attracted to the timeless and beautiful Scandinavian aesthetic and way of life. I hope you enjoy this armchair tour through Nordic lands, culture, and arts. I hope the projects are a feast for your eyes and hands, and that they add notes of Scandinavian beauty to your own home.

ACKNOWLEDGMENTS

Deep and heartfelt thanks to my friends, the designers and teachers who created the projects in this book. Thanks to the National Nordic Museum and the American Swedish Institute for sharing their collections with me and the public, and most especially to Vesterheim Norwegian-American Museum and its chief curator, Laurann Gilbertson, for their support and folk art teaching programs. Thanks to the fiber arts vendors who contributed to the projects: Glimakra USA, Halcyon Yarn, The Yarn Guys, Vävstuga, and Blue Heron Knittery in Decorah, Iowa, one of my favorite yarn stores on the planet.

Thanks to John and Veronna Capone for lending their gorgeous photography of Scandinavia to this project; to my friend Sarah for lending her time, camera, and artistic eye; and to my husband, Job, for more project photography technical support and for buying those professional studio lights that I gave him such grief about at the time.

Thanks to my friends and family who cheered me on. Thanks to cousin Anne Berit, who drove down to the family cabin on Oslo fjord to take pictures for me. Thanks to my editor, Sandra Korinchak, not least for her PBS mystery recommendations to keep up morale. And, finally, thanks to Linda Ligon, ever the Pied Piper, who decided that I should write this book.

Scandinavia is known around the world for its quality of life and for an aesthetic that is cutting edge and modern yet rooted in tradition, nature, and artisanal skills. From tapestry and garments, jewelry, and carving dating back to Viking times to the transformational aesthetic of mid-century modern design and the paradigm-shifting work of modern Scandinavian designers and leaders, the Nordic countries are a model for lovers of art and culture. That's why Nordic fiber arts, from knitting to felting and weaving, have been a core part of the craft scene for decades. (I have American knitting books of my grandmother's from the 1940s that prominently feature Nordic patterns for the fashion-conscious American.)

The book takes you on a tour of Nordic fiber arts as a part of Nordic culture. Each chapter explores a set of values that are core to Scandinavian life and how they are reflected in the customs and folk arts of different Nordic regions and in Scandinavian history. The projects, many based on traditional folk art, explore these same cultural values through design, material, and techniques.

The projects are mainly household textiles (no sizing or fitting required!) that add a bit of Scandinavian spirit to your home or make great gifts. They can be made with tools that fit into most crafters' budgets, and I have specified the yarns that were used, but you can substitute yarns of similar weight and texture if you prefer. There are step-by-step instructions to help beginning fiber artists achieve beautiful results and to entice experienced crafters to try new techniques or combine them in new ways.

Because this is an armchair tour, there are no schedules, and no planes or trains or boats to catch. You can come back to this book again and again, perhaps tempted by a new technique each time or finding a different aspect of Nordic life that resonates with what's happening in your own (or that you long for in your own). You can read, make, explore as your curiosity and time allow. The point is to enjoy the journey.

And I hope it is a journey of discovery. Just as Scandinavians were the first Europeans to sail out of sight of land, voyages made possible by their sleek hand-hewn ships, I hope that with this book and your hands, you can cast off from familiar shores, finding adventures that give your heart joy.

Góðr vegr!
(Old Norse for "Good travels")

CHAPTER ONE

IN SEARCH OF SCANDINAVIA

Opposite: Scenery near Lofoten, Norway. Photo by John Capone.

Above left: Hallgrimskirkja, a Lutheran Church in Reykjavik, is named after Icelandic poet and clergyman Hallgrimur Petursson. Photo by John Capone.

Above right: View through window of a relocated building in the Jämtli Open Air Museum, Östersund, Sweden. Photo by John Capone.

What is it about Scandinavia that draws our imagination, admiration, and, often, imitation?

In America, where I live, even friends who have no Scandinavian ancestry sometimes tell me they have decided to be "Scandinavians of choice." Iceland is the hip destination for many millennials I know, the Danish *hygge* craze had a good run, to the delight of candle vendors everywhere, and the fashion and décor conscious are yet again embracing "Scandi style." Nordic fraternal organizations are thriving, and people many generations removed from "the old country" turn out to enjoy Midsommar and Nordic festivals, often in folk costumes that their ancestors would have recognized. (By the way, I generally use the word "Nordic" to describe the region or culture and the word "Scandinavia" to refer to the countries.)*

The work of Nordic hands certainly draws us in. When you think of Scandinavia, along with images of fjords or Vikings, I'll bet your mind's eye conjures up brightly painted Dala horses, gleaming pewter bowls, or fine-knit Norwegian sweaters and Finnish mittens. Or maybe you imagine more modern Nordic craft: the bent wood of a mid-century classic Alvar Aalto armchair, bright stoneware designs from Finland, runway fashions from "Scandi style" designers such as Maline Berger and Henrik Vibskov, or iconic nature-inspired fabrics from Marimekko. And we love to make Nordic-inspired things. Viking reenactors can be spotted hand-spinning and smithing at medieval summer "faires," Nordic craft classes and conferences fill quickly, and enthusiasm for Scandinavian crafts long preceded and has outlasted the peak of the "maker" movement.

---

*Strictly speaking, the Nordic countries consist of Denmark, Finland, Iceland, Norway, and Sweden and also include the Faroe Islands and Greenland (autonomous regions of Denmark) and the Åland Islands (autonomous region of Finland). Scandinavia consists of Norway, Sweden, and Denmark.

So, what is the appeal of all things Nordic? I think the answer lies partly in myth, partly in reality, and partly (to paraphrase Shakespeare) not in our North stars but in ourselves. In other words, each of us may be drawn to different aspects of Scandinavian culture and crafts, and what draws us may change over time. This book offers you many ways to explore these rich cultures and craft traditions, and to find your own answers.

That said, I think there are values and ways of living, arts, and aesthetics that are truly Nordic, and they contribute something unique and important to the world. So, let's start our journey with a whirlwind tour of Nordic lands, history, and people, both myth and fact, to find the origins of Nordic character, culture, and craft.

(Don't worry. This mostly a cultural history, so I will spare you the litany of dates and wars and the endless succession of rulers named Harald, Haakon, Christian, or Gustav, punctuated by the occasional Olaf.)

IN THE BEGINNING: THE NORDIC LANDS

The history and character of the Nordic countries spring from the land. It is a place of extremes: from Norway, with its snow-clad mountains and deep fjords, to Denmark, where the tallest "mountain" is 171 meters (561 feet) high; from the barren volcanic beauty of Iceland to the dense forests of Finland and the inviting farmland of Sweden; from ice-covered Greenland to the windswept Faroe Islands and the maritime beauty of Åland. While many factors have shaped the Scandinavian peoples, their story begins with the land.

All the Nordic countries except Iceland are perched on the Fennoscandian or Baltic shield, part of an ancient continent, which was scoured by the advance and retreat of Pleistocene glaciers. Later upthrust activity created the southern Swedish highlands, parts of Greenland, and the Scandes, the mountainous backbone of the peninsula containing Norway and Sweden. The land is dotted with lakes left by the last ice age, which ended about 12,000 years ago.

All five Scandinavian countries have territory within the Arctic Circle (Denmark by virtue of its ties to Greenland), where darkness lasts from October to March, and much of the land can be covered with snow and ice many months a year, as shown in the satellite photo.

Fortunately, the climate of Scandinavia is moderated by the surrounding waters—the Atlantic Ocean and the Baltic, Barents, Norwegian, and North

In this mostly cloud-free photo, much of Scandinavia can be seen to be snow covered in March 2002. From left to right across the top of this image are the countries of Norway, Sweden, Finland, and northwestern Russia. The Baltic Sea is at bottom center, with the Gulf of Bothnia to the north and the Gulf of Finland to the northeast. Image courtesy Jacques Descloitres, MODIS Land Rapid Response Team at NASA GSFC—Moderate-resolution Imaging Spectroradiometer (MODIS), flying aboard NASA's Terra satellite.

Thingvellir National Park, Selfoss, Iceland. A rift valley formed by the North American and Eurasian tectonic plates drifting apart. Photo by John Capone.

Seas—and, most importantly, the warm flow of the Gulf Stream. To understand the benefits of the Gulf Stream, consider that the average January low temperature at Trondheim, Norway, is a pretty tolerable 26° Fahrenheit, while the average mid-January temperature in Noyabrsk, Russia—at essentially the same latitude—is −17° Fahrenheit.

Most soil consists of glacial deposits, a grayish-yellow mixture of sand and rocks topped by a thin layer of humus—not a planting mix designed to make farmers rich. Most of Scandinavia has little arable land, ranging from around 7% in Finland to a paltry 1.2% in Iceland. The exception is Denmark, with almost 60%. However, the surrounding seas and marine-influenced climate have provided Scandinavia with abundant fish and forests, making life possible in these far northern realms.

AN ABRIDGED HISTORY OF SCANDINAVIA

The First Scandinavians

Regular human habitation in Scandinavia began around 10,000 years ago, as Paleolithic reindeer and seal hunters followed their prey north in the wake of the retreating glaciers.[1] Over the next five millennia, more hunter-gatherers moved up the west coast of Norway and then into Sweden and Finland as the ice retreated farther and the land rose. (For part of this period, the Baltic was actually a giant freshwater lake, filled by glacier melt.) Recent genetic research suggests that the Sámi people, the only recognized Indigenous population in Europe, first migrated into what is now northern Finnish Lapland before 8100 BCE.

Rock carvings in Alta, Norway, dating back to 4200 BCE. Photo by John Capone.

Stone Age dwelling at Kierikki Stone Age Centre. Photo by Ninaras, Helsinki, Finland, licensed under CC BY 4.0.

Klekkende Høj is the only double-passage tomb found on the island of Mons in Denmark. The island has over 119 megalithic tombs, of which about 38 are protected sites today. Photo courtesy of Professor Phillip Charles Lucas, Stetson University.

View out the left (east-facing) entry of Klekkende Høj. Photo courtesy of Professor Phillip Charles Lucas, Stetson University.

The Trundholm sun chariot, now in the collection of the National Museum of Denmark, is the most famous artifact of Bronze Age sun worship in Scandinavia. Photo by National Museum of Denmark, licensed under CC BY-SA 3.0.

The second wave of immigrants, beginning in the third millennium BCE, had adapted to new climatic conditions, bringing agriculture, stock animals, the first permanent settlements, pottery making and toolmaking, horses, and the practice of burying their dead in passage graves and mounds (to the undying gratitude of today's archeologists).

By the Bronze Age (1500–500 BCE) the inhabitants of Scandinavia were trading amber, furs, and other goods for copper and tin from central Europe and as far away as the Iberian Peninsula. Graves from this age have preserved some of the oldest woolen textiles still in existence. These largely agricultural people worshiped the sun, whose precious presence enabled life in the North. In celebration of it, their culture left metalwork and stone carvings that, according to historian T. K. Derry, derived artistic motifs from as far away as Mycenaean Greece "and not infrequently improved upon its borrowings."[2]

In the final years before the Christian era, classical civilization began to notice the North. Pliny the Elder and Tacitus referred to the area north of Jutland, now part of Denmark, as "Scatinavia." (According to Derry, "Scandinavia" came from a misreading of Pliny's manuscript.)

"The Fury of the Norsemen"

In January 793, the Vikings, the modern name used for the seafaring Norse raiders and traders of the period, burst into European history with an attack on the wealthy English abbey at Lindisfarne. For the next two centuries, in their fast, sleek ships, the Vikings spread across Ireland, the Hebrides, northwestern Germany, the Low Countries (present-day Belgium, Luxembourg, and the Netherlands), and northern France. They settled permanently as dukes in Normandy, colonized Iceland and the Faroe Islands, and established the Danelaw across much of northwestern England. They raided, took slaves, and, according to Derry, committed deliberate acts of cruelty to keep subject populations in check. The Irish prayer "From the fury of the Northmen deliver us, O Lord" (*A furore Normannorum libera nos, Domine*) reflected real fears.[3] But Derry notes that they were more than raiders. Where they found land unoccupied, they settled, and when they could not raid, they were eager to trade.

The Vikings are often romanticized or sanitized in popular culture: from heroic Ragnar Lothbrok in the popular historical drama *Vikings* to the benign comic strip about a Viking, *Hagar the Horrible*. In fact, the Viking chieftains were products of a brutal age. They were less remarkable for their ferocity than for succeeding in their invasions without the large armies and resources of the Romans, Greeks, and other conquerors. The wealth and labor they brought to Scandinavia, whether through pillage and enslavement or trade, also brought a flowering of Scandinavian arts, with elaborate metalworking, wood and stone carving, and ornamental weaving and embroidery, adding to the homely arts of spinning and weaving household cloth.

Christianity, Kings, Commoners, and Crafts

The Vikings came in contact with Christianity during their travels through Europe, often adopting local religious practices where they settled. By the end of the Viking era, many Scandinavians mixed some Christian ideology with their old Norse pagan beliefs. Around the beginning of the eleventh century, mindful of the power of the church to move against them and also of potential alliances with Christian monarchs, the Viking chieftains began to convert to Christianity. (They often expressed their newfound Christianity by killing other people who declined to convert. So, once a Viking, always a Viking.)

For centuries after the Viking period, the borders of the Scandinavian countries were in flux. Sweden and Denmark struggled with each other for control of the Baltic, and parts of Norway and Finland were conquered and traded between Sweden and Denmark. Iceland paid tribute to whoever controlled Norway at any given time.

In the fifteenth century, the Scandinavian kingdoms began, in fits and starts, to convert to the Lutheran faith. Among the common folk, conversion was inspired by German Lutheran missionaries. Among the nobility and royals, it was sometimes inspired by study at Lutheran centers in Germany and sometimes by potential alliances with other Lutheran rulers.

During the Middle Ages and Reformation, the lot of the common people—the farmers, fisherman, woodcutters, and artisans—would worsen or improve, depending on which of the Scandinavian monarchs laid claim to their region, whether the monarch du jour found it convenient to favor the commoners or nobles at any given time, how much money that ruler needed to raise for the war(s) of the moment, and whether they were likely to be conscripted for said wars.

But, by the end of the eighteenth century, the lives of rural Scandinavians began to improve. By then, Finnish peasants and Icelandic farmers were typically freeholders instead of serfs. The Swedish peasantry gained land and rights, and by the early 1800s, 60% of the land worked by Danish and Norwegian peasants was peasant-owned.[4]

Over these centuries, as the power struggles among the Vikings gave way to the power struggles among nation-states and then nations, the common people

Left: The Oseberg ship on display at the Viking ship museum, Oslo. Photo by Petter Ulleland, licensed under CC BY-SA 4.0.

Right: Detail, the Oseberg ship. Photo by Karamell, licensed under CC BY-SA 2.5.

in Scandinavia, in addition to scraping out a living, were evolving a body of folk art and craft as distinct and lovely as any in the world. Increasing security and prosperity allowed those arts to flower, and the prior centuries of shifting national borders created folk art styles and techniques that were regional rather than just national. We see household furniture and interiors dating back to the Reformation with the beautiful floral painting known as *rosemaling* in Norwegian and "kurbits" painting in Sweden. (The iconic wooden Dala horses of Sweden are an example of kurbits.) There is beautiful carving, from lintels and furniture to household items. There are woven coverlets from farmhouses, many painstakingly woven on warp-weighted looms that could be disassembled to save indoor space when not in use. And as the Scandinavian countries moved into the industrial age, these folk arts became not only a pleasure to their makers and owners but also a powerful symbol of emerging Nordic identity.

Weaving in progress on a warp-weighted loom, Maihaugen Open Air Museum, Lillehammer, Norway. Photo by John Capone.

Rosemaled drinking bowl. Collection of Vesterheim Norwegian-American Museum, Decorah, Iowa.

Nation Building and National Identity

By the mid-nineteenth century, Europe began to be transformed by nationalism—a shift from monarchical rule, with boundaries set by royal alliances and conquests, to the idea of nation-states with distinct national identities. Aligned with and supporting this political movement was a cultural and artistic movement called national romanticism, which valued imagination and sentiment over reason, and often romantic fiction over fact, and which sought to build national identities from stories of a virtuous and heroic past. The Swedes formed the Gothic Society, which celebrated a heroic, albeit mythical, Gothic past. The Norwegians set about separating their national language from Danish, Finnish art drew inspiration from their national epic, the *Kalevala*, and the Icelanders went mad for lyrical poetry. (Interestingly, Victorian Britain also went crazy for Viking themes in the arts at this time, taking national pride in a highly romanticized Norse heritage.) The Danes and Norwegians also expressed their love of country through landscape painting that emphasized the inspiring beauty of Nordic nature, as seen through the lens of national pride. (The fjords in paintings became more dramatic than real life, the farms more pastoral, the bluffs along the Danish coast far higher, etc.)

By this time the Nordic countries were on their way toward urbanization and industrialization. In reaction, the Arts and Crafts movement spread from Britain to Scandinavia, aiming to bring art into the home with beautiful design, high-quality materials, and the joy of craftsmanship. The paintings of Swedish artist Carl Larsson celebrate this ideal, with images of pastoral peace and domestic bliss,

A Danish Coast. View from Kitnæs on Roskilde Fjord, Zealand. Johan Thomas Lundbye, 1843. In the collection of the National Gallery of Denmark.

The Kitchen (Ett hem åt solsidan). Carl Larsson, probably 1848. In the collection of the National Museum of Sweden.

woven through with elements of folk art such as a floral-painted kitchen cabinet, a handwoven rug, or children dressed for Christmas in traditional folk costumes. Perhaps because the Industrial Revolution came late to Scandinavia, coinciding with the rise of national identity, its people never lost their appreciation for craftsmanship and traditional handwork.

The Scandinavian Exodus

While the Nordic countries can be portrayed in today's popular culture as egalitarian, progressive, and almost utopian, it's worth remembering, as historian Mart Kuldkepp observes, that "throughout centuries, the Nordic region has much more commonly been a place that people have wanted to leave."[5] He cites the Jutes' invasion of the Western Roman Empire and, of course, the centuries when Vikings made themselves a "Europe-wide nuisance." But the greatest period of exodus from Scandinavia extended from the nineteenth century through the Second World War, when over three million Scandinavians moved abroad, driven by poverty and population pressure. And the majority of these Nordic émigrés came to America.

In the nineteenth century, nutrition and healthcare improved throughout Europe, and infant mortality dropped (the potato was as great a nutritional gift to Scandinavia as to Ireland). Between 1800 and 1914, the populations of Denmark, Norway, and Sweden tripled. The growing rural population struggled trying to survive on the fixed and small amount of arable land. Conditions for factory workers in the cities were often as bad or worse, with long shifts, low pay, and shanty towns for housing.

America beckoned, with the promise of land for the settling—security, prosperity, and, as migration continued, ready-made communities of one's countrymen with whom to associate. And that was important because, in a time of rising nationalism, Nordic emigrants weren't seeking to trade away their Scandinavian identities for opportunity.

So much of that identity was reflected in the folk arts and crafts they brought with them. The early settlers would bring a spinning wheel, a rosemaled chest, or a coverlet received as wedding presents. They might bring linens, Hardanger lace or embroidery of couples in a wedding procession, and *skillbragd* coverlets, blankets with a special overshot design that were given at weddings and christenings. And, of course, the *bunad*, the folk costume that was worn for national days and holidays.

By the late nineteenth and early twentieth centuries, many of the Scandinavian emigrants—including my own grandparents—were young, single people seeking opportunities. They would join an existing community of their countrymen in America and meet prospective spouses at Scandinavian social clubs or churches, as my own grandparents did. When they married and set up housekeeping, it would be a Scandinavian household, with all the traditions and trappings thereof. My grandmother came to America with very little to her name, but, like many emigrants and their children, in the 1950s and 1960s she went back to the "old country" when she could. And every trip, she would bring back more Scandinavian handwork to fill her home, often of a quality she could never have afforded as a girl in northwestern Norway. More coverlets and other handwoven textiles, rosemaled trays, hand-painted stoneware bowls, embroidered linens, and hand-knit sweaters for the family, plus pictures and paintings, often in the Romantic

Clockwise from top left: Antique spinning wheel from Gudbrands-dalen, in the author's loving care.

Table mat in Hardanger lace, date unknown. Hardangersom dates to the 17th century in Norway. Collection of Vesterheim Norwegian-American Museum, Decorah, Iowa.

Bunad, typical of Fana, Hordaland, in the Norwegian Institute of Bunad, Valdresmusea, Fagernes, Norway. Photo by John Capone.

Detail of a skillbragd coverlet from More og Romsdal, Norway, ca. 1855–1888. (In Sweden, this technique is called opphämta.) Collection of Vesterheim Norwegian-American Museum, Decorah, Iowa.

tradition. She was proud of the lives she and my grandfather had built in America, but when one visited her home, there was no doubt that she was Scandinavian to the core.

SCANDINAVIA TODAY AND THE NORDIC BRAND

The Nordic countries maintained neutrality through the First World War, but World War II proved an existential threat to Norway, Denmark, and Finland. To ensure access to Swedish iron ore for its war efforts, Germany occupied Denmark and Norway. In the meantime, Finland was invaded by Russia, then made a brief, ill-fated alliance with Germany in order to reclaim its territory. The fortunate Icelanders were defended first by the British and then by the Americans, with the added benefit of being able to sell supplies to those garrisons. Only Sweden stayed neutral, selling ore to the Germans while also taking in some refugees from its Nordic neighbors.

After the war, the Nordic countries decided to band together for mutual benefit. The Nordic Council of Ministers, formed in 1952, includes Denmark, Finland, Iceland, Norway, Sweden, the Faroe Islands, Greenland, and the self-governing Finnish province of Åland. In addition to cooperation on social and environmental issues, Nordic Council initiatives include international public relations for the Nordic region, originally to help their economies recover after the Second World War. Some of our stereotypes of Scandinavia (what sociologists call "autostereotypes") come out of these very intentional and effective Nordic branding efforts.

Initially, the council was aiming to build recognition and demand for Nordic products. Today, those branding efforts also involve tourism promotions full of magnificent fjord vistas and photos depicting a pastoral paradise, with snug farmhouses and cabins. One Viking Cruises commercial that runs on my local public broadcasting station features an apple-cheeked, white-haired grandmother baking ginger cookies for the tourists, in traditional folk costume, of course.

There's also a perennial perception of "Scandi-cool." When I was growing up, Scandinavian design was all the rage, from architecture to furnishings to fashion. Many families I knew had a freestanding Scandinavian fireplace in their homes, the bright, enameled Nordic cross between a chiminea and a flying saucer, often with a very "mod" rya rug in front of it. Mid-century modern furnishings were known to Americans as Danish modern (an unintentional slight both to the German Bauhaus movement and the Finns, who were such innovators in mid-century design).

Today, the Scandi-cool image is still associated with innovative, minimalist design. (There's even an interior design style called Japandi, a fusion of Japanese and Scandinavian aesthetics breathlessly described as "minimal, functional, warm, and calming, with touches of wabi-sabi enthused [sic] imperfection."[6] As my grandmother would have said, "Uff da!") Contemporary Scandinavian fashion designers also combine functionality with elegance and, often, a touch of

Exhibit of Danish Modern furniture in the Design Museum, Copenhagen, Denmark. Photo by John Capone.

tradition. But the touch of cool also comes from Nordic noir novels such as Stieg Larsson's *Girl with the Dragon Tattoo* trilogy, and from Scandinavian popular music, ranging from ABBA to Björk to bands that combine electronic rock with New Age and, of course, Viking elements.

The Nordic countries are also portrayed as more socially progressive, more environmentally conscious, and consistently happier than most. Much of that reputation is deserved. The Scandinavians see their social democracies as a "middle way" between socialism and unbridled capitalism. The Nordic countries provide healthcare and education, paid family leave, and high-quality daycare for all citizens. Yet, capitalism also flourishes in these countries, and, despite high taxes, global companies such as Maersk, IKEA, and Nokia thrive there.

The Nordic countries are also leaders in protecting the environment. Norway set a deadline for climate neutrality by 2030 and leads the world in electric vehicles per capita. (Only slightly ironic, considering the extent to which recent Norwegian prosperity is built on North Sea oil.) Denmark has already cut carbon emissions by half in this century, and over half of its electricity now comes from wind power. And Iceland, taking advantage of its volcanic geography, is a leader in geothermal and hydrogen power.

Finally, the Scandinavian countries consistently rank at or near the top in the World Happiness Report[7] and the World Happiness Index.[8] Both reports base their rankings on factors such as economic health, life expectancy, social support, freedom, and public charitable giving. Yet, the Nordic nations have many of the same problems as everyone else: high costs of living, political polarization, and conflict over growing immigrant populations. So, what makes the Scandinavian people so consistently happy? And how can the rest of us get some of that? Well, that's what this book is all about.

Steel-work panel in the museum yard, Kulturen Center, Lund, Sweden. Photo by Veronna Capone.

TRUE NORTH: CRAFTS FOR A NORDIC LIFE

In many ways, Scandinavia's history is not so different from that of the rest of northern Europe, from Stone Age hunter-gatherers to the emergence of nation-states and industrialization. But Scandinavians have a special approach to life that is forged by the North. (As the American humorist Garrison Keillor says of Minnesotans, "We are a northern people.")

In the Far North, nothing is taken for granted, and adaptation is critical. The first Scandinavians survived by following the retreating glaciers in search of food, then turned to farming and fishing as the glaciers retreated farther northward. They have always made the most of the resources at hand, from wood and wool to the power of wind and water. They value both tradition and innovation: they don't abandon what works, but they know that to adapt is to survive.

Scandinavians know the value of scarce resources, quality rather than quantity, and making things to last. They value self-reliance and the work of their own hands, and they also know the importance of banding together, whether to get through a cold Nordic winter or to succeed as nations in the modern world. And because life can be hard, they know how to enjoy the good things: the beauty of the land, the sun when it shines, the everyday pleasures of community, surrounding oneself with a few beautiful handmade things, or just having a good cup of coffee and a chat.

In 2021, an article in *Slate* magazine claimed to reveal "The Grim Secret of Nordic Happiness."[9] The author, a Finn who now lives in Michigan, argues that Finland—the 2021 "Happiest Country in the World"—and the other Scandinavian nations rank as happy only because they have reasonable expectations of life. Well, having reasonable expectations doesn't seem grim to me. It seems like common sense. But I think the other, bigger secret to Nordic happiness is having the right priorities—valuing nature and community, the work of one's hands, and the simple qualities of one's life.

Those are the values we're going to explore in the chapters ahead, through the arts and customs of Scandinavia and through projects designed to bring a little Nordic happiness to your hands and home.

CHAPTER TWO

NATURE IN NORDIC LIFE

Lofoten, Norway. Photo by John Capone.

Gökotta: To have a picnic at dawn to hear the first bird's song

Kura skymning: Sitting quietly pondering dusk

Smultronställe: "Wild strawberry place." A special place for relaxation, free from stress.

Sommarmorgon: Summer morning

—Swedish words about nature

For people who live in a pretty harsh environment, Scandinavians have a surprising and abiding love affair with the nature around them. As the British writer Michael Booth[10] points out, industrialization in Norway did not lead to urbanization as it did in other countries, so people there have always lived closer to the land. Still, the Scandinavian thirst for the outdoors is singular. They revel in the outdoors, and not just in the glories of the midnight sun, but also in the dark depths of the Nordic winter. Tracing the footsteps of the first Scandinavians, who followed the retreating glaciers rather than rest in warming southern climes, today's Scandinavians take every opportunity to enjoy their natural environment and to bring it indoors through their folk art.

Photos of Norwegians
living the *friluftsliv*.
Collection of Vesterheim
Norwegian-American
Museum, Decorah, Iowa.

Mid-summer night celebrations, Maihaugen Open Air Museum, Lillehammer, Norway. Photo by John Capone.

LIVING THE FRILUFTSLIV

For Norwegians, being outdoors is a national passion. It even has a name: *friluftsliv*, meaning "open-air living." The term was coined by the Norwegian playwright Henrik Ibsen in his 1859 poem "On the Heights," at the height of the National Romantic period. But the love of outdoor living has been part of Norwegian culture for centuries, and it endures today. As *National Geographic* noted in a 2020 article, "The idea is as Norwegian as cross-country skis and aquavit."[11]

Friluftsliv is a commitment to spending time experiencing and appreciating the outdoors, no matter the weather. In Norway, this can mean hiking, skiing, swimming in a fjord, spending time with friends around a beach bonfire, or hunting trolls like the father-daughter "troll-hunting" team featured in the *National Geographic* article mentioned above. (This particular open-air child has spent more than three hundred nights of her scant five years sleeping in a tent. To date, father and daughter haven't captured any actual trolls.) The website Visit Norway reports that it's common for Norwegians to go hiking or cycling on a first date. Some universities offer a degree in friluftsliv, and there's an ancient and now-modern law, *friluftsloven* (*allemansrätten* in Sweden and *jokamiehenoikeas* in Finland), which grants people the right to roam anywhere, provided they respect the land and the landowner's privacy. The Norwegians even have a word, *utepils*, for drinking a beer outside. So, you can see that friluftsliv doesn't always require athletic prowess or camping gear.

In my family, friluftsliv translated to skiing in all weather and a lot of very soggy hikes in the Cascades. ("But the mountains are beautiful in fog and rain.") There were also soggy fishing trips ("The fish bite better when it's raining."), exciting sailing adventures in storms and howling winds, and my father's oft-intoned and very Norwegian pronouncement that "there's no such thing as bad weather; only bad clothes." So, as kids, we were well clothed in wool, nature's miracle fiber, from our long underwear to our Norwegian sweaters.

GLAD MIDSOMMAR: WELCOMING THE LIGHT

In lands with so many months of winter dark, it's natural that summer is enjoyed to the fullest, and summer celebrations kick off with midsummer festivals in the Nordic countries. Before the Viking conversion to Christianity, the summer solstice festivities celebrated a fertility rite and the triumph of the returning light over winter darkness. As Christianity was adopted, the celebration came to be associated with the feast of Saint John the Baptist. Modern Swedes celebrate

An old mountain hytte. Photo by Felix Mittermeier from Pixabay.

Midsummer's Eve on whichever Friday falls between June 19 and 25, and *midsommar dag* the next day. In Norway and Denmark, it is called *Sank Hans Aften* and is celebrated on June 23, the evening before the feast of Saint John. Finns celebrate the feast of Saint John, *Juhannus*, on the Saturday between June 20 and 26. (In Finland, this feast was originally a tribute to Ukko, the god of thunder.) Icelanders call the holiday *Jonsmessa* (John's feast), and they celebrate on June 24.

Midsummer traditions abound in the Nordic countries. The festivities can begin with families heading to the forest to pick flowers and make wreaths. In some areas, people dress up in traditional costumes and dance around maypoles. The weaving of the maypole ribbons takes skill, and as different ages participate (and as beer may flow), hilarity can ensue. I was lucky enough once to be in Dalarna, Sweden, for midsummer, where we enjoyed the local competition to lift the biggest maypole —definitely a fertility rite!—and seeing the ladies from Mora win the Viking boat races, as they do every year (at least, according to one Mora woman's proud husband).

All the Scandinavian midsummer celebrations ultimately include bonfires as the center of the feasting, singing, dancing, and socializing. At the midsummer feast, strawberries, salmon, and pickled herring are eaten to celebrate summer's bounty, and of course there's plenty of beer and aquavit, just because. Campfire bread dough called *snobrød*, *pinnbröd*, or *pinnebrød*, depending on the country, is wrapped around skewers and cooked over the flames, then eaten with hot sausages, giving children formative campfire cooking experience for their future version of friluftsliv.

There are also lots of folk traditions around the magical midsummer time. In Sweden, it's said that if a girl picks seven types of flowers on her way home on

Midsummer's Eve and sleeps with them under her pillow, she'll dream of a future husband. Icelandic tradition says that on midsummer night, cows can talk, seals can transform into humans, and good health can be won by rolling naked on the dewy grass in the midnight sun. However, if you sit all night at an intersection where all four roads lead to churches, elves will appear to seduce you with food and gifts. (Given the sparse population of Iceland, I suspect there are few intersections that qualify, so the elves are probably disappointed most years.)

ESCAPE TO THE HYTTE

Home is where the heart is, but to Scandinavians, the vacation home—be it cabin, cottage, or hut—is where the happy is. Many Scandinavian families have a second dwelling where they go for weekends and vacations, summer and winter. In Norway, it's called the *hytta* or *hytte*, and in Sweden, the *stuga*. The Finns have *mökki*, the Danes have *sommerhus*, and in Icelandic, it's a *sumarhús* or *sumarbústaðir*. The typical cabin is small, built of wood, and snug rather than luxurious. It can be at the coast, as my family's is, or in the mountains. It may be a holiday home with electricity and plumbing, or it may truly be just a wooden fisherman's hut or ski hut.

Norway is best known for its "cabin culture," but many Swedes and Danes have vacation cabins on the Baltic, and Finns have long headed to cabins in the forest for peace and solitude. (Of course, a Finnish cabin should have a sauna.) Icelanders are apparently obsessed with their summer cabins: if their family doesn't have one, they can rent one from their labor union. Today, new vacation cabins in Scandinavia are often prefabricated, designed to be exquisitely efficient

and compact and to fit with the landscape, so nature can be enjoyed with minimal
The important thing about a hytte is not the building but what happens there.
People truly unplug from work and tune into nature, family, and friends. Most
of the day is spent outside, swimming, skiing, hiking, napping in the sun, or just
socializing while enjoying the sun and sounds of the outdoors. Meals happen
outdoors whenever possible, and everyone pitches in on cooking, cleaning, and
other chores. *Hytter* are passed down through families, a place where every generation can bond with nature and with each other.

BRINGING THE SUMMER IN: ROSEMALING BY MANY NAMES

Today the floral painting style known as *rosemaling* ("rose painting") in Norway
and *rosmålning*, *dalmålning*, or *kurbitsmålning* in Sweden has become emblematic of
Scandinavian folk art. The famous wooden Dala horses are painted in this style,
and their images now bedeck everything from woolen blankets and dish towels
to IKEA candles. Rosemaled furniture and household items are handed down
in families and treasured by collectors. The art is being practiced and refined by
today's artisans, including stunning pieces I've seen by rosemalers of Japanese
heritage. Pieces by well-known rosemal artists and rosemaled pieces in Scandinavian
import stores fetch premium prices.

Rose painting is actually a fairly late addition to the Scandinavian craft tradition, although decorative painting in churches dates back to the Middle Ages.
In the late seventeenth and early eighteenth centuries, artists were brought from
other areas of Europe to paint churches in the baroque and later rococo styles,
and Scandinavian artisans learned the techniques by copying the European styles
or studying abroad. Wealthy landowners commissioned these artisans to paint

Left: Dala horses, an example of the Swedish *dalmålning* painting style. Photo by Nick Sieger, licensed under CC BY-SA 2.0.

Right: A 1799 painting with kurbits ornamentation, by Winter Carl, at Danielsgården, Bingsjö, Sweden. Photo by Frode Inge Helland, licensed under CC BY-SA 2.5.

the walls and ceilings in their homes with the lush floral paintings, sometimes combined with landscape scenes.

Slowly, the technique was copied by rural craftsmen, often added to their other skills such as woodcarving or carpentry. In the 1700s, the typical farm family in the poorest parts of Scandinavia, such as northern Norway, lived in a windowless cabin with a central fireplace and smoke hole in the ceiling. (Norwegians called this an *årestue*, meaning "open-hearth room.") The only light came through a rain covering above the smoke hole, a cow stomach stretched over a wooden frame. Farm families in more prosperous areas of Scandinavia might have a second room for storage and a tiny window or two, but always there would be the open hearth. Painted walls were not for the rural poor, because paint was expensive and, besides, ornamentation on the walls would soon have been covered with soot. But rural people began to bring summer inside with painted bowls, chests, and drinking vessels.

By the late eighteenth and early nineteenth centuries, as land reforms improved the lot of rural farmers, the dark, smoke-filled *årestue* gave way to more

Interior of Rygnestad *årestue*, Stesdal, Norway. Photo by Karl Ragnar Kjertsen, licensed under CC BY-SA 4.0.

comfortable dwellings with fireplaces, chimneys, and at least a few glass windows. At the same time, the Industrial Revolution made good-quality paint affordable, and as the light poured into the new farm dwellings, so did the painted flowers, covering walls, fireplaces, beds, cabinets, and more.

Over time, distinct styles of rose painting developed in different areas. In Norway, the three main styles are Telemark, known for its flowing, asymmetric designs; Hallingdal, with large, symmetric flowers and simpler scrollwork; and Rogaland, symmetrical like the Hallingdal style, but more ornate. In Sweden, the kurbits (meaning "gourd") painting style, with light brushstrokes depicting gourds, leaves, and flowers, flourished in Dalarna and southern Norrland. In fact, the saddle design on a Dala horse is actually a gourd motif.

While the popularity of rose painting subsided after its peak in the 1850s, it never disappeared, thanks to a combination of nostalgia for the "old country" and good old Nordic branding. As Scandinavians immigrated to America, they took their cherished rose-painted household items with them to remember their former homes. As these pieces were passed down, they sometimes faded and needed restoration by fellow emigrants who had

Rambergstugo at Heddal Bygdetun. Photo by Lisa Amalie Elle, licensed under CC0 1.0.

Rose-painted child's chair, made by Per Lyse, 1935. Collection of Vesterheim Norwegian-American Museum, Decorah, Iowa.

Opposite: Trunk with Telemark-style rose-painting, Sogn, Norway, 1860. Collection of Vesterheim Norwegian-American Museum, Decorah, Iowa.

rose-painting skills. During the Depression, Per Lysne, an out-of-work carpenter who had immigrated to Wisconsin from Laerdal, Norway, began doing restoration work on people's rose-painted heirlooms and then producing new items for sale. Lysne's work and teaching sparked a rose-painting renaissance in America, one that continues today through an active rosemaling community and through teaching programs, the best known at the Vesterheim Norwegian-American Museum in Decorah, Iowa.

The branding story comes from the now-iconic Dala horse. Originally, the little horses were toys, carved by Dalarna foresters for their children and painted in "Falun red," a paint color made with tailings from copper mines in the region. But by the late 1800s, the Falun mine was in decline, and many people emigrated in search of work. At the same time, Sweden, in its modern, nation-building phase, adopted Dalarna as the "Swedish heartland." The Dala horse found its way into the paintings of Carl Larsson, whose paintings depicted an idealized Swedish domestic life, and Dala horses found their way into the homes of urban Swedes yearning for the romantic pastoral life. In early-twentieth-century Swedish children's books, wee ones even rode magical Dala horses on Christmas Eve adventures to fairyland, tying the toys to the yuletide celebrations.[12] The business of making and painting Dala horses provided work for farmers and foresters, and at least one Dala horse factory is still in business today.

NATURE IN NORDIC DESIGN

Nature is never out of style in Scandinavia. The Nordic countries have a continuous tradition of nature-inspired design, from rose painting and carved floral designs through the Arts and Crafts movement of the late 1800s, twentieth-century art nouveau and mid-century modern, and on to today's world-renowned Scandinavian architecture and "Scandi style."

Ishavskatedralen (Arctic Cathedral), Tromsø, Norway, a beautiful example of Nordic architecture that brings nature in. Photo by John Capone.

The minimalist, nature-inspired look we associate with Scandinavian design was first brought to the world's attention by an interior design show that traveled through the US and Canada in the mid-1950s. It featured the style we call "mid-century modern," which was called "Danish modern" by my parents' generation. Today, the hallmarks of high-end Nordic interior design are the use of natural materials—wood, stone, natural fibers, leather—and uncluttered space with muted natural colors that reflect the Nordic landscape, ideally flooded with natural light. Lines are graceful and elegant, and spaces are spare but never cold. Bright colors are used sparingly and spectacularly, like flowers dotting the landscape in a Nordic spring, and old can mix harmoniously with new.

The bright spots in contemporary Nordic interiors are often the textiles, and perhaps the Nordic textiles most recognized around the world, besides Scandinavian sweater patterns, are the nature-inspired prints of Finnish design house Marimekko. Marimekko was founded by Finnish textile designer Armi Ratia in the aftermath of World War II. Finns couldn't afford imported clothing or textiles, so Ratia and her husband turned their oil-cloth printing business to printing her own designs on fabric. From its first fashion show in 1951, Marimekko quickly grew to an international design brand and became part of Finland's national identity while it recovered from the ravages of the war. Marimekko fabrics, with bold, organic shapes and bright, abstract flowers, came to be known the world over. I remember my mother's excitement when she was able to purchase a yard of the fabric (not cheap, even then) and frame it for our wall. Of course, I visited the

Marimekko's famous Unikka print. © Alexander Rauch Photography, "50th anniversary of Unikko," Creative Industries Styria.

Marimekko store when I was in Helsinki, a pilgrimage for a kid raised on mid-century design, and took pictures for Mom. Marimekko has brightened many a home and business for over seventy years, and some of the designs from the 1950s and 1960s, such as Unikko/Poppy, are still in production today.

NORDIC SUMMER AND WINTER THROW

by ANITA OSTERHAUG

CRAFT: *Knitting*
DIFFICULTY LEVEL: *Intermediate*

This cozy throw is knitted in two-color brioche stitch—not a traditional Scandinavian style of knitting, but the effect is very Scandinavian modern in its simplicity, and I find the multicolored patterns reminiscent of the traditional krokbragd hangings that I love to weave.

The colors on one side of this throw are inspired by Nordic summers—the green of new grass, the blue green of sun through seawater, and the sweet blue of spring flowers. The other side pays tribute to Nordic winters, with brilliant snow, dark-gray stone, and the shimmering black of a sky shot through with Northern Lights. (As in nature, the summer side of this throw begins and ends in the shimmering dark of the winter sky.)

The pure Icelandic wool yarn in this project is also a miracle of nature: lustrous and warm, yet light as a feather. I recommend starting this throw in early fall, so it can keep your lap warmer and warmer as the weather turns colder and the knitting grows.

Structure: Brioche knitting

Materials
Yarn Lopi Léttlopi (100% Icelandic wool; 109 yd [100 m] / 1.75 oz [50 g]):

Winter C1: #1707 Galaxy, 4 balls

Winter C2: #0051 White, 6 balls

Winter C3: #9418 Stone Blue Heather, 3 balls

Summer C1: #9423 Lagoon Heather, 5 balls

Summer C2: #1404 Glacier Blue Heather, 5 balls

Summer C3: #1406 Spring Green Heather, 4 balls

Needles Size 7 (4.5 mm): 47" circular (cir). Adjust needle size if necessary to obtain the correct gauge.

Notions Markers (m); tapestry needle.

Gauge 16 sts and 14 visible rows = 4" in brioche st (where Row 1S + Row 1W = 1 visible row).

Dimensions
Finished Size: 76¾" long by 40" wide.

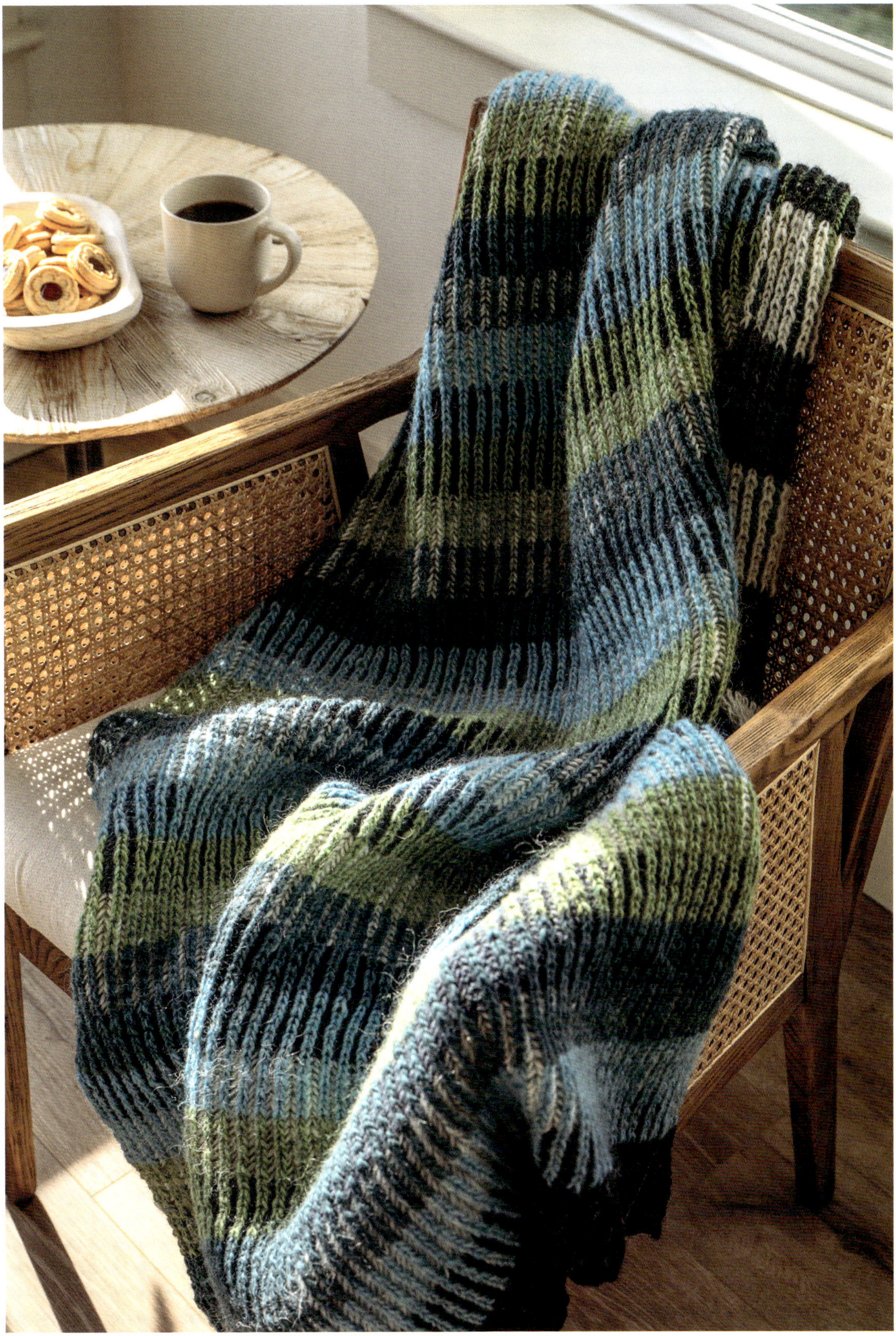

Notes

- This throw is worked back and forth in 1-color and 2-color brioche stitch.
- In 2-color brioche knitting, you work two rows for each side of the fabric, one color following the other. So, you work the first color on your circular needle, then slide the stitches to the right and work across with the other color, then turn and work a row of each color for the other side.
- On the chart, each color is used for 8 rows (where Row 1S and Row 1W together count as one row), but either the Summer or the Winter color is changed every 4 rows so that the changes are staggered. After working 8 rows of a color, there will be 8 visible knit stitches of that color in the work.
- To weave in ends for finishing, thread end on a tapestry needle and sew back along its path several columns into the fabric, wrap end around (above and below) top of stitch of the same color, then tear yarn, leaving a wispy end that you can tuck behind the stitch.

Reverse side

Stitch Guide

Slip 1 yarnover (sl1yo): Sl 1 pwise wyf, yarn over needle to back. If next st is brp, after bringing yarn over needle to back, bring yarn between needles to front.

Brioche knit (brk): Knit st tog with its companion yarnover.

Brioche purl (brp): Purl st tog with its companion yarnover.

Single-color brioche (even number of sts): Row 1: *Brk, sl1yo; rep from * to end. Rep Row 1 for patt.

Two-color brioche (even number of sts): Row 1S (Summer color): *Brk, sl1yo; rep from * to end; do NOT turn work. Slide sts to other end of needle.

Row 1W (Winter color): *Sl1yo, brp; rep from * to end; turn work. To create first sl1yo, sl first st, then bring new color from back of needle between end st and next st, then bring it over needle and to back, then between needles to front to purl. (This keeps the other color from wrapping around the outside of the edge stitches.)

Figure 1. Yarn Color Order

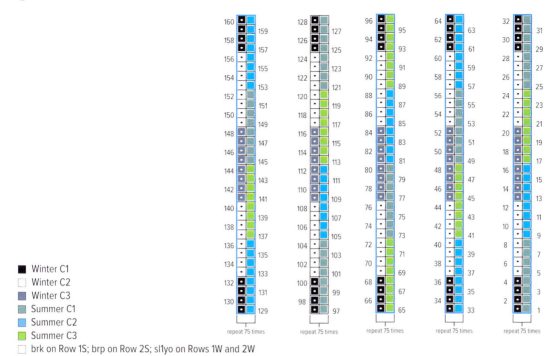

- ■ Winter C1
- □ Winter C2
- ■ Winter C3
- ■ Summer C1
- ■ Summer C2
- ■ Summer C3
- □ brk on Row 1S; brp on Row 2S; sl1yo on Rows 1W and 2W
- · brp on Row 1W; brk on Row 2W; sl1yo on Rows 1S and 2S

each odd-numbered row represents Rows 1S and 1W
each even-numbered row represents Rows 2S and 2W

Row 2S (Summer color): *Sl1yo, brp; rep from * to end; do NOT turn work. Slide sts to other end of needle.

Row 2W (Winter color): *Brk, sl1yo; rep from * to end; turn work.

Rep Rows 1S–2W for patt.

Instructions

With Winter C1 and using the long-tail method, loosely CO 150 sts.

Set-up row: *K1, sl1yo (see Stitch Guide); rep from * to end.

Work Single-color Brioche (see Stitch Guide) for 13 rows.

Working in 2-color Brioche (see Stitch Guide), work Rows 1–96 of color chart 2 times, then work Rows 1–64 once more (see Notes).

With Winter C1, work Single-color Brioche for 13 rows.

Next row: *Brk, p1; rep from * to end.

Loosely BO all sts so that your throw can stretch and drape over you.

Finishing

Weave in ends. You don't have to block the throw, but blocking does help to even out stitches and remove any dirt from knitting. Whenever you need to wash it, handwash in warm water with mild soap, then roll in a towel to squeeze out excess water and lay flat to dry.

GLACIER: A COZY RUG FOR THE HOME OR HYTTE

by SARAH SHIPPEN

CRAFT: *Knitting*

DIFFICULTY LEVEL: *Advanced beginner*

I chose Lopi Plötulopi unspun wool yarn, from Icelandic sheep, for its excellent felting properties and for its rustic character that reflects Iceland's rugged landscape. Part of the pleasure of making this rug is winding the yarn from the cakes of singles into the 8-strand working yarn. Don't view this as a chore! The winding will progress quickly and will help you get comfortable with the hand and delicacy of the Plötulopi yarn. Your hands will learn to soften their grip on the yarn, allowing you to knit with the relaxed tension needed for this piece. Once the final balls are wound, the rug will knit up very quickly.

The rug is knitted in linen stitch because it will lie flat and, once fulled, is a thick, cushiony surface. The knitted rows run the length of the rug; hence the 47"–60" circular needle. With the exception of the cast-on and bind-off tails, all ends are worked in with felted joins, so when the knitting is done, the rug is nearly finished! This rug is also reversible. You can choose which texture you prefer to show: the smooth woven-look knit side or the pebbly purl side. It is not a hard-wearing rug for a high-traffic area, but, rather, one you will want next to your bed or a favorite reading chair so you can snuggle your toes in its soft, nubby surface.

Materials

Yarn Lopi Plötulopi (100% Icelandic wool; 328 yd [300m] / 3.5 oz [100g]):

- **C1:** #2023 Light Blues, 1 cake
- **C2:** #0003 Light Beige, 2 cakes
- **C3:** #1026 Light Ash Heather, 2 cakes
- **C4:** #2025 Gulf Stream, 2 cakes
- **C5:** #1431 Arctic Blue Heather, 1 cake
- **C6:** #1432 Winter Blue Heather, 1 cake

Needles Size 17 (12 mm): 47"–60" circular (cir). Adjust needle size if necessary to obtain the correct gauge.

Notions Tapestry needle; digital kitchen scale with gram units; calculator; 4 small bowls for winding yarn; 24" by 36" rug pad (optional).

Gauge 5 sts and 12 rows = 4" in linen st, before fulling.

Dimensions

Finished Size: Before fulling: 48" long by 28" wide. After fulling: 39" long by 25" wide.

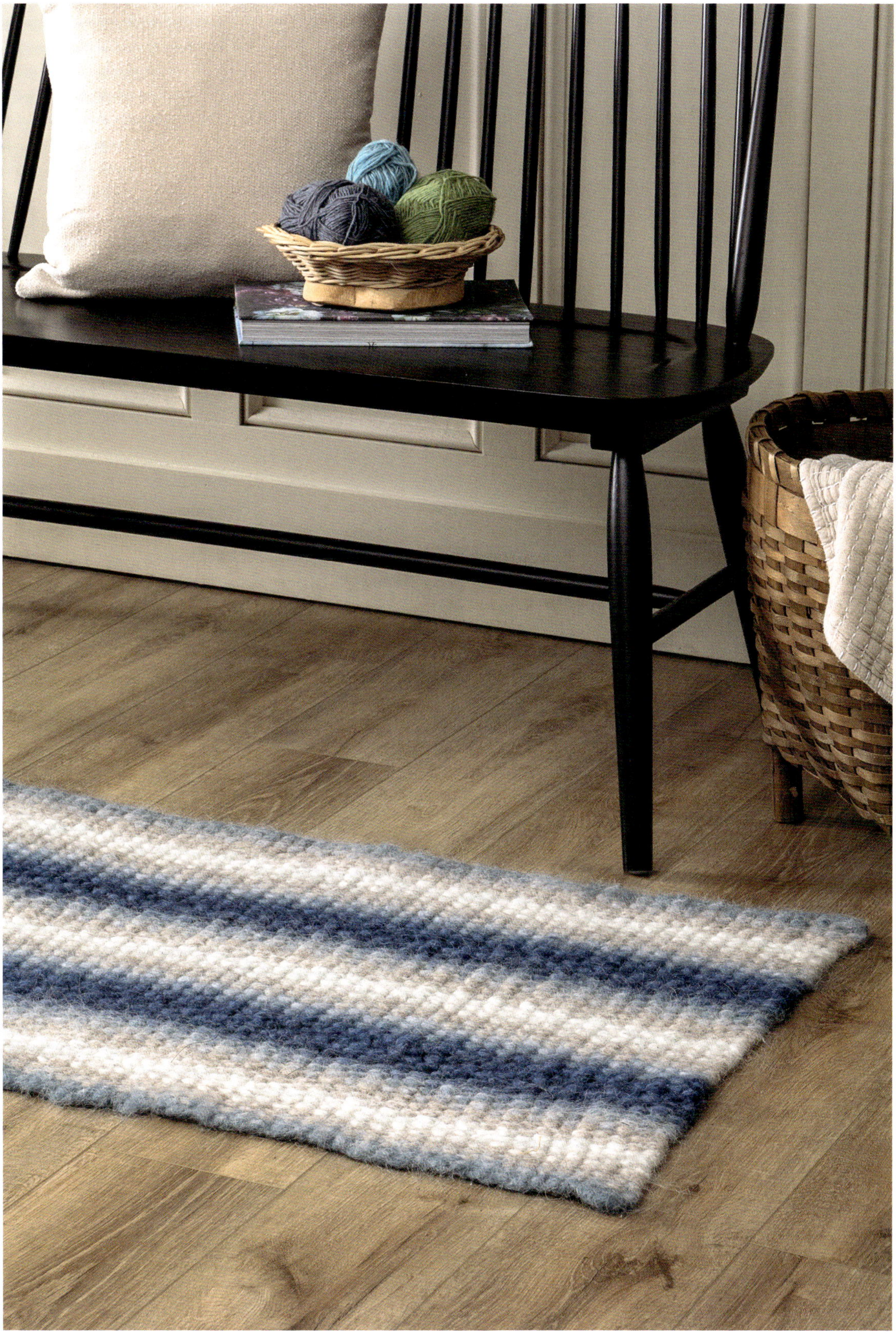

The colors and texture of this knitted rug are inspired by the rugged beauty of Iceland's terrain. I designed the rug to reflect Iceland's snowy peaks, rocky crags, and the deep blue and aqua ice of its glaciers.

View of Virkisjokull and Falljokull glaciers as seen from route 1, Iceland. Photo by Francis92.

Notes

- This rug is worked back and forth with eight strands of yarn held together throughout.
- Felted joins with Plötulopi yarn: When you change colors in this rug, you will felt the yarn ends together so that the joins don't show, and you won't have lots of ends to weave in during finishing. To prepare for felting, add one or two drops of soap to 2–3 ounces of water in a small bowl and keep it next to you while knitting. Four stitches before the end of a wrong-side row, in anticipation of a color change, break the yarn by pulling it apart to leave a 6-inch tail with wispy ends. (Don't cut it!) Pick up the new color yarn and overlap tails 3"–4" in the palm of your hand (see photo **1**). Wet your fingertips and sprinkle the overlap with two or three drops of water. Starting slowly with gentle pressure, rub the two tails between your palms, increasing speed, until they start to felt (see photo **2**). Rub with increasing pressure along the join for ten to fifteen seconds more until ends are felted together (see photo **3**). Don't worry if the join isn't extremely strong: it only needs to be strong enough to hold together to knit with, and you can knit with the yarn while it is still moist. The fulling will felt these joins in place in the finished rug, and they are much tidier and easier than weaving in ends later!
- All color changes happen at the end of wrong-side rows. With linen stitch, the working yarn always wraps around the end of the row to create a smooth finished selvedge. Even tension is essential for an attractive finished rug. As you knit, practice keeping the tension even and the edges straight and making sure that the yarn wraps smoothly as you turn the work. Do not tighten too much or you will distort the edge.
- With linen stitch, the floats from the slipped stitches are all on the right side of the piece. It is a simple stitch, but similar enough to k1, p1 ribbing that your hands may fall into old habits. Check for mistakes often. With the large gauge of this pattern, they will show.

1. Overlapping tails for join.

2. Felting the join.

3. Felted join.

Stitch Guide

Long-tail cast-on (LTCO) with Plötulopi Yarn: The cast-on stitches for this project need to be evenly spaced on the needle, and spaced widely enough that there is no drawing in at the cast-on edge. To achieve this on the very thick yarn, place your right thumb and index finger in front of the last cast-on stitch on the needle and cast on the next stitch against your thumb to maintain consistent spacing. Tighten the stitch gently against your thumb, being careful not to shorten the spacing (see photo **4**).

4. Spaced long-tail cast-on.

Linen stitch (even number of sts): Note: Always wrap working yarn around selvage at end of row.

Row 1 (RS): *K1, sl 1 pwise wyf; rep from * to end.

Row 2 (WS): *P1, sl 1 pwise wyb; rep from * to end.

Rep Rows 1 and 2 for patt.

Yarn Preparation

You'll need to prepare the 8-strand yarn before you knit your rug. It's a simple, fun process. First you wind strands of the yarn from each cake together into 2-strand balls, then you'll wind those together to make the 8-strand yarn.

The cakes are 100 grams minimum, but they frequently weigh a bit more than this, so you'll need to weigh them before you start winding. Use the kitchen scale to weigh each yarn cake in grams, and record the weight.

For each color, wind four balls of doubled yarn. There are two cakes of colors C2, C3, and C4, so divide the weight of each cake by 2. For colors C1, C5, and C6, divide the weight of the single cakes by 4. Record these numbers.

Wind 2-strand balls: To begin, set a yarn cake on a towel on the floor and then find both ends of the yarn: the one on the outside of the cake and the one in the middle. This unspun yarn is delicate and will break if yanked, so be especially careful when pulling the end out from the center of the cake.

Gently pulling both ends, start wrapping the two strands together into a soft ball (see photo **5**). If one of the strands breaks, don't worry! Just overlap the ends about 6" and rub briskly between your palms to create a soft, felted join.

Weigh the ball frequently and stop when you reach the target weight you calculated for that color. Set this ball aside and start winding the next ball. Continue until you finish the yarn cake(s) for that color.

Wind 8-strand balls: To begin, put the four 2-strand balls of yarn for one color into four bowls and set them on the floor. While standing, take the end of a doubled strand from each ball of yarn and wind together into a large ball, creating an 8-strand yarn to knit with (see photo **6**).

Repeat for each color.

You are now ready to knit!

Left: 5. Winding 2-strand ball of pencil roving.

Right: 6. Winding a 4-strand ball.

Knitting a Sample Mini Rug

It's important to get the tension right so that your rug will lay flat, so I recommend practicing linen stitch and the other rug techniques with some surplus Plötulopi yarn by first making a mini rug. You have enough of colors C3 and C5 to make both the sample and the full-sized rug.

With C5 and using the long-tail method (see Stitch Guide), CO 10 sts.

Set-up row (WS): Work Row 2 of linen st (see Stitch Guide) to last 4 sts, break C5 and make felted join with C3 (see Notes), work in patt to end.

Rows 1–8: Work in linen st with C3. Make felted join with C5 4 sts from end of Row 8.

Rows 9 and 10: Work in linen st with C5.

BO all sts.

Weave in ends in middle of sts for 3"–4" along CO and BO edges.

Sample rug.

Figure 1. Yarn Color Order

Instructions

Note: You will need a tail about 3⅓ yd long for the CO. With C1 and using the long-tail method (see Stitch Guide), CO 60 sts.

Set-up row (WS): With C1, work Row 2 of linen st (see Stitch Guide) to last 4 sts, break C1, leaving a 6" tail, make felted join with C2 (see Notes), cont in patt to end.

Beg with Row 3 of Rug Color Sequence, work linen st through Row 82 of Rug Color Sequence, changing colors as described in Notes.

With RS facing, BO all sts using standard BO, checking BO tension after each st to ensure that BO st sits directly on top of st below. (For rug to lay flat, there can be no stretching or tightening of piece at edge.) Use a larger needle to ensure proper spacing if necessary. After binding off, break yarn, leaving a 6" tail, pull to taper it, and use a tapestry needle or crochet hook to work in the tail along and under the BO edge.

Finishing

Using warm water and a small amount of gentle soap, such as Dreft, fill the tub of a top-loading washing machine one-third full. Set the machine to heavy agitation, add a couple of pairs of jeans or other lint-free garments to aid in fulling, then add the rug and start the washer. Agitate for twenty to thirty minutes, checking often. The piece should be fulled so that the wool binds together and you cannot poke your finger through the stitches, but not so hard it becomes stiff and misshapen. The tension should stay relaxed enough that it will lay flat on the floor. Once the rug is sufficiently felted, spin out the soap and rinse gently in warm water, then spin dry. Lay out on a beach towel and use blocking pins if necessary to dry it in an even rectangle.

If you're placing your rug on a smooth floor, use a 24" by 36" rug pad underneath to minimize wear and keep it from slipping.

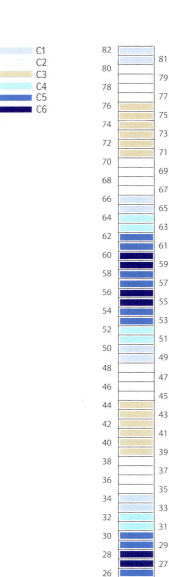

A Telemark Bouquet

by LAURA BERLAGE

CRAFT: *Needle felting*
DIFFICULTY LEVEL: *Beginner*

The basics of rosemaling can be learned with a few days' instruction, but the skills are mastered and refined over a lifetime. For those of us who love rosemaling but express ourselves in fiber, here is a rosemaling project that we can paint with wool!

This piece is inspired by rosemaling pieces in the collection of the Vesterheim Norwegian-American Museum and was designed in collaboration with Vesterheim Folk Art Competition Gold Medalist rosemaler Patti Goke.

Ale bowl with Telemark-style rose-painting, Øyfell, Telemark, Norway, either 1807 or 1867. Collection of Vesterheim Norwegian-American Museum, Decorah, Iowa.

Technique: Needle felting

Equipment
Foam block or padded work surface that you can poke needles into (to protect your table or leg). An old towel folded up will work in a pinch.

8-inch embroidery hoop

38 gauge 3-sided felting needle. You can use the needle by itself or with a handle, if you prefer.

Sharpie or another cloth marking or transfer method

For finishing: 8-inch round frame (glass removed), extra wool or fiber fill to pad the fabric. You could also choose to display this piece in the embroidery hoop.

Materials
9" by 12" piece of felt in a soft blue. Either craft felt or wool felt is fine.

Wool roving, in deep blue, sky blue, natural white, red, yellow, and moss green, about 0.2 oz of each color. (See the Resources for information on ordering supplies from Laura's farm, North Star Homestead.)

Dimensions
The design is 8" in diameter. The piece can be framed as a circle, as an oval, or in a square frame.

Telemark Needle Felting Pattern (80% of actual size)

Tips for Needle Felting

- The pattern is shown at 80% of actual size. Enlarge as you like to fit your fabric.
- As you work, rest the embroidery hoop on top of the foam block or padded work surface on a sturdy table. Do not try to hold the hoop up in your hand while you work, as you might in traditional embroidery. It's too easy to poke yourself with the needle!
- Make sure to hold the felting needle with good posture. I use a three-point grip between my thumb and middle finger, then use my index finger as a "bump stop" to keep the needle from slipping or wobbling. Also, poke the needle straight in and out to avoid breaking it.
- With wool-style needle felting, it works best to pull off very small amounts of wool from the roving, laying them on one at a time. Always pull the wool apart with your fingers; never cut it, because that will create thick, blunt ends that are difficult to hide later.
- Periodically, pause during your work to make sure that the back of your piece isn't getting too felted into your foam or padded work surface. This is also a good time to check the backing to see if it needs to be retightened.

1. Stretch felt fabric in embroidery hoop.

2. Work main scroll, then add accents.

3. Finish with greenery, flowers, and fine white lines.

Instructions

Draw or transfer pattern onto the felt fabric, being careful to center it on the fabric.

Stretch the felt in the embroidery hoop, making it snug (see photo **1**). Check that the design is still within the circle of the hoop, so it can easily be worked. (Keeping the fabric snug will make the felting process much easier and ensure that the fabric doesn't pucker. You may need to retighten the backing occasionally during the felting process.)

Painting with wool is rather like doing an oil painting—you work the colors and shapes farthest away from the viewer first, and the colors and shapes closest to the viewer last. So, start with the main scroll in the design, working with the yellow at the "root" (base) of the design. Laying on one small piece, first felt around the edge of the shape, then poke down the middle. When adding a second piece, make sure that it overlaps with the first, so the color saturation is even. If you can still see the backing color through the wool, add just a little more. In needle felting, it is always easier to add more wool. It's quite difficult, on the other hand, to take wool off once it's well felted in!

Once you've worked the main scroll in yellow all the way up to the top nob, come back to the "root" and work the deep blue part of the scroll (see photo **2**). Use fine amounts of wool as you come along the side of the "C" shape. For the curl-off to the right, start at the nob and then work it back to the scroll, blending the fibers with the rest of the deep blue. Add white and sky-blue accents and hints of outlining by drafting thin bits of wool off the end of the roving and felting these in. Flick the tip of the needle to spread out the fibers and create a feathered, brushlike texture for shading.

Next add greenery, then flowers, and, last, the fine white lines that tie the elements together (see photo **3**). For lobed shapes such as the leaves, work each lobe as a separate small piece of roving, folded over in a teardrop shape. For round shapes such as the cinnamon roll or "lollipop" flowers, roll the wool in your hands to form a ball, then felt it onto the backing. For spirals, start at the center and work outward. For small balls, focus on the outer edge, allowing the center to remain slightly puffy. You can experiment with allowing some elements to retain more height (by felting them less), while making other elements flatter.

Feel free to bring your own interpretation to this design. Every rosemaler has her or his own flair, color preferences, and style. Be inspired by rosemaled examples you've seen, and make this piece your own!

BRIGHTLY FINNISH FLOWERS

by CHRISTIANE PAYTON

CRAFT: *Felting*
DIFFICULTY LEVEL: *Beginner*

The initial inspiration for this wet-felted oven mitt came from Norwegian rosemaling. But I indulged my own preference for warm earth colors and went with a bolder yet still-traditional color scheme. The cheery shapes and soft, earthy colors remind me of the bright simplicity of a Finnish rya rug or a Marimekko print. For your mitt, you can follow my design or invent one of your own.

Techniques: Wet felting and needle felting

Equipment
Foam block or padded work surface that you can poke needles into (to protect your table or leg). An old towel folded up will work in a pinch.

38 gauge 3-sided felting needle. You can use the needle by itself or with a handle, if you prefer.

Plastic or metal tray with rim for wet-felting work area

Plastic quilting template or other strong, flexible plastic for mitt template

Small bucket for felting water

Mild non-detergent soap such as Eucalan or Dreft

Large piece of bubble wrap

18"–24" piece of dowel or pool noodle (optional)

Materials
Wool roving, in light and dark orange, cornflower and teal blue, and leaf green (or colors of your choice), about 2 oz of each color, plus 8 oz of blue or color of your choice for the oven mitt itself.

Sewing thread to match the color of the oven mitt.

Dimensions
Finished mitt: About 13" long by 7½" wide.

1. Tools for felting.

2. Begin felting the mitt.

3. Felting the underlayer.

4. Pre-felt squares.

5. Pre-felt shapes.

6. Laying out the design.

Making the Shrinkage Sample

Make a test felt sample to determine the shrinkage rate of the wool you're using for the project:

1. On top of a tray or other waterproof surface, layer "tiles" of roving in four layers, alternating direction with each layer, in the shape of a 10" square.

2. Sprinkle with warm, soapy water, then rub and work the wool until it is felted and stable, but not stiff. Start gently and work more vigorously as the sample felts.

3. Set the felt in a warm place to air-dry.

4. Measure the finished sample and calculate the shrinkage in each direction from the original 10" square. For example, my 10" square had shrunk to 8" in length, a shrinkage rate of 20%.

Instructions

1. Put a favorite oven mitt from your kitchen stash on paper, trace its outline to make a template, and take measurements. Then apply the shrinkage rates from your test sample to increase the size of the template. For example, if your oven mitt is 9" long and the shrinkage rate is 20%, your template will need to be 10.8" long to allow for shrinkage. Also, decide what colors and shapes you want to use in your design on the mitt (in my design, there is a "call and response," meaning that color combinations are repeated in several areas to create a cohesive design).

2. Using the new measurements, enlarge your mitt template on the basis of the new measurements, then cut out a larger mitt template from tarp plastic.

3. Begin felting the mitt on a waterproof work surface. I used a plastic tray to keep the water from going all over the place during the felting process. Cover your surface with a piece of thin plastic film. Place your plastic template on your work surface and carefully build up four layers of tiled wool roving on it, alternating vertical and horizontal orientation with every layer, and making sure to extend the roving layers about ½" past the edges of the template.

4. After all the layers are in place, gently sprinkle warm, soapy water all over the roving tiles and gently press down on them with your hand to get rid of air bubbles and to allow the water to thoroughly wet the wool (see photo **2**). (Go easy with the water, though. You don't want the wool swimming in a puddle.) Next, carefully flip the template over so that the wool layers are now underneath the template rather than on top.

5. Fold the excess wet wool roving over the edges of the template and proceed to build up another four layers of roving on this side of the template (see photo **3**). All edges of the template should now be covered with wool roving, including the bottom edge where the hand will eventually be placed into the mitt. The opening will be cut open later in the felting process. Sprinkle the new layers with soapy water, then press them with your hand as before to get out bubbles and wet the wool.

6. Once both the front and back layers of the roving tiles are thoroughly wet through, fold the thin plastic over the project and begin to rub gently in a circular pattern. This helps the fibers start to bind to one another, while at the same time not sticking to your hand. Rub first one side of the mitt and then the other, making sure to rub the edges of the mitt where the two layers come together and overlap.

7. After five minutes of gentle rubbing on each side, test the fabric by pinching the surface of the wool and pulling up to see whether the fibers are sticking together: resistance means that the fibers have started to stick to one another. If they aren't felting, you may need to use warmer water or rub more vigorously (or both). Once it is felted enough to hold together, set the mitt aside to dry for a day. (This fabric is not felt yet, since the fibers are not locked together. This stage is called prefelt.)

8. Next, make prefelt rectangles of various colors for the surface design of your mitt (see photo **4**). Make these as you did the original felt sample, but work them only to the prefelt stage by gently rubbing the surface of the thoroughly wetted wool until the fibers begin to stick together. When the prefelt rectangles are ready, set them aside for a day to dry.

9. When your colored rectangles are dry, cut out flower and leaf shapes to decorate your mitt (see photo **5**). Cut them larger to allow for the same percentage of shrinkage as with the mitt fabric. Loosely needle-felt any details you like onto the cutout shapes.

10. Place the design shapes where you want them on the oven mitt and lightly needle-felt around the edges just to hold them in place (see photo **6**). Next, wet down the mitt plus design with warm, soapy water, pressing gently to work the water in, then cover it with plastic film in order to keep the design in place. Rub gently in circular motions to felt the design onto the mitt without dislodging the design pieces. After several minutes, check to see if the desired felting is taking place. Once you can tell that the design pieces will stay in place, rub more vigorously to lock the design onto the mitt and to continue felting the mitt itself.

11. When the mitt is fairly stable, finish the felting process by putting the wet mitt on a large piece of bubble wrap, then rolling it up so that the bubble wrap encloses the entire piece, with no edges exposed. To hasten the final felting, you can wrap the mitt plus bubble wrap around either a wooden dowel or a piece of pool noodle so that there is some resistance in the middle of the roll. Using your forearms, roll the project on your working surface forty times. Unroll the project, flip it over, and repeat the rolling action. Repeat the rolling with the project wrapped lengthwise, widthwise, and on the diagonals so that the fabric is evenly felted from all directions. At this point, the shrinking will happen more rapidly, and you will notice that the mitt has shrunk down so much that it is causing the tarp plastic template to bend significantly on the inside of the project. Once that happens, use a sharp pair of scissors to cut open the bottom of the mitt where you would put your hand in, then pull out the template.

12. Continue to felt down the project, first with the rolling action and, finally, by throwing the bunched-up mitt down with considerable force onto a hard surface (I do this in my utility sink to avoid splattering water all over the place). After the template has come out, make sure that the insides of the mitt do not stick together during the continued felting process. Periodically turn it inside out that you can felt the inside more. Once your mitt has the approximately correct dimensions, you can spot-felt (rub) in specific areas to get it to the exact shape that you want.

13. When you are pleased with the final look and dimensions of your project, rinse it multiple times and then squeeze out as much water as possible to hasten the drying process. I shaped my mitt over my hand and then put it over a heating register, and it dried within twenty-four hours. If you want to make any "edits" once it's dry, you can wet the project again with soapy water and spot-felt to make those changes (for instance, I decided to add a thin layer of a contrasting color to the inside of my mitt).

14. To make the braid for the cuff, attenuate several strips of roving of your desired color, wet them with soapy water, and prefelt them by lightly rolling them as you would a play-dough snake. Once they're prefelted, braid the three strands together, then continue to felt the braid until it's fully felted. Dry the braid, needle-felt it to the cuff, then sew it on with matching thread.

CHAPTER THREE

THE VALUE OF COMMUNITY

Above left:
Celebrating Lucia Day
in Sandviken, Sweden.
Photo by ferrantraite
via iStock.com.

Above right: Danes
gathered at the
beaches around the
small island of Atilde
to celebrate Easter by
boiling eggs in
seawater on bonfires.
Photo by Morten
Kjerulff via iStock.com.

*A lone fir in an open field withers away. A lone man loved by none,
how can he live?*

—*Viking saying from the Eddaic poem* Hávamál

Social interactions are one of the paradoxes of Nordic culture. Cozy Nordic traditions such as *hygge* are much admired and emulated by those of us in other cultures, yet Scandinavians are also sometimes described as reserved, aloof, or even cold. In fact, a study by Expat Insider[13] found that out of sixty-five countries, Norway, Denmark, and Sweden held the bottom three spots for ease of making friends, with Finland coming in at fifty-seventh.[14] Yet, community has been a cornerstone of Nordic life since ancient times. So, do Scandinavians, like their seasons, run warm and cold?

Speaking from my own experience, both in Scandinavia and at home, friendship, family, and community are the foundations of Nordic culture. Scandinavians consider it impolite to bother other people, and that can make them seem standoffish. But if you ask them for help, you'll get it, and once you get to know them, they tend to be sociable, generous, and kind. To see how Scandinavians value community and fellowship, you need only look at their traditions. But first, we need to talk about *Janteloven*.

THE STRANGE LAWS OF JANTE

In 1933, a Danish-born novelist named Aksel Sandemose wrote a novel that includes a small Danish town called Jante, in which everyone is expected to follow ten rules for social behavior.[15] The "laws of Jante" dictate a kind of humility that seems pretty oppressive to a twenty-first-century American. For instance, an individual must not think that they are special, are good at anything, or can teach others anything, or that anyone cares about them. Sandemose's characterization of Jante is satirical, and he doesn't present its social code as a model for society (Sandemose himself was no moral model, reputedly engaging in questionable business practices and changing countries when his deeds caught up with him).

Nonetheless, the laws of Jante, or *Janteloven*,[16] are famous to this day because they captured certain social norms in Scandinavia. Sandemose himself wrote that many Scandinavian readers told him they recognized their own hometowns in his novel.

I never heard of Janteloven growing up, but I was certainly taught never to tout my own accomplishments or consider myself better at anything than anyone. (There is a Swedish proverb: "Noble deeds are done in silence.") When I finally read about Janteloven, I asked a Norwegian friend whether it was really a thing in Scandinavia. My normally cheery, easygoing companion got a fierce look in her eye and intoned, "Yeeew are not better than anybody else, and don't yew think yew ARE!" Which I interpreted as "Yes, it's a thing."

Some scholars put this Scandinavian standard of self-effacement down to Lutheranism. Personally, I question whether Lutheranism shaped Scandinavia or Scandinavians adopted Lutheranism because it fit with their lived experience. Certainly, survival in a harsh land required a certain dedication to the collective good. Modern Scandinavians have a love-hate relationship with the Jantian ethic. Some argue that it discourages individual excellence, but other scholars also credit Scandinavia's high levels of equality, standards of living, and world happiness rankings to their culture of putting the community first.

Janteloven aside, Nordic people highly value friendship and togetherness. If they seem reserved at first, it is because they are unassuming, and they don't assume you want to talk to them. So, it may be up to you to make the first move. And perhaps it's my own Nordic reticence speaking, but in our culture of personal

Left: Mock battle at the Viking festival in Hafnarfjörður, Iceland. Photo by HalliHuberts via iStock.com.

Right: In Helsinki, crowds celebrating after Finland won the International Ice Hockey Federation's world championship. Photo by VikaValter via iStock.com.

Kardemummabullar are a staple of fika in Sweden. And they are delicious! Photo by Ann-Britt Nilsson from Pixabay.

"brands" and oversharing, a little more humility and privacy might not be so bad. But once you're past the reticence, you'll find Scandinavians to be plenty social.

THE SOCIAL RITUAL OF COFFEE: FIKA, IN MANY FORMS

One of the quintessential Scandinavian forms of togetherness is gathering over coffee or tea and something sweet to eat. The group can be friends, family, or coworkers, and the occasion can be formal or informal, scheduled or spontaneous. The point is to stop, relax, and connect with others. The best-known word for this, one that's becoming familiar outside Scandinavia, is the Swedish word *fika*. In Denmark, the word is *bica*, in Iceland, *kaffitímar*, and Finns call it *kahvi*. Norwegians simply say "*Skal vi ta en pause?*" ("Shall we take a break?") and everyone knows it's time for coffee and conversation.

Fika has a rich history in Sweden. Cookbook author Brontë Aurell relates that in the late 1800s, elaborate coffee parties spurred bakerly competition among housewives. And after the deprivations of the second World War, a now-classic Swedish cookbook, *Sju Sorters Kakor*, gathered hundreds of options for the seven kinds of cookies a hostess would offer her guests for fika. During Nazi occupation, Danes were allowed to meet in public only to share coffee and food, so community *kaffebord* (cake tables) became a cover for resistance meetings.[17]

Today, fika can be as simple as inviting a friend for coffee at home or in a café. Meeting for coffee can also, as in other countries, be low-key date activity. It can also be a family gathering with food and cake that goes on all evening. My Norwegian grandmother had her own word for fika: visit. Only it was pronounced like two words, "vi sit," and the second part was pronounced as in "Sit yourself down." In Grandma's later years, my Aunt Katy helped her with her finances,

People socializing in the square of Faaborg, Denmark. Photo by stigalenas via iStock.com.

and I often went with Katy to Grandma's house. On the way, we would stop at the Scandinavian bakery to buy cookies or a pastry, and Grandma would have the coffee on when we arrived. The first words out of her mouth were always "Let the paperwork be for a bit. Now you sit down so we can visit." In my parents' home, too, we were always prepared for friends or relatives to drop in, with a supply of homemade cookies and coffee at the ready. Nordic humility is all very well, but hospitality is a matter of pride!

Fika also happens at work. Workers in Scandinavia don't grab a coffee to go and then work nonstop while it gets cold on their desks. Businesses have coffee breaks built into the workday; good coffee is served in a cafeteria or break room, often with a sweet of some kind, and people actually take time out to savor it and chat. Coming from the culture of the American high-tech industry, I was impressed when I visited the Dale of Norway factory near Bergen and saw the whole staff converge on the cafeteria for *kaffen*. Coffee and cookies appeared and everyone—from managers and supervisors to the ladies running the knitting machines—settled down to socialize. In my job at that time, managers would have looked disapprovingly at anyone sitting down for a coffee break, but in Scandinavia, it was considered smart to give people a rest, build relationships, and promote good morale.

BUNADS, GROUP SINGING, AND OTHER SIGNS OF SOLIDARITY

Scandinavians love to socialize, and Nordic culture teems with group activities. In *The Almost Nearly Perfect People*, the British writer Michael Booth recounts the Danish mania for belonging to clubs, societies, and other groups, from

Children in national dress walking in a parade on the 17th of May, Norway's Constitution Day. Photo by Ranveig Thattai, public domain, via Wikimedia Commons.

birdwatching to sports to what Americans would call cosplay (costumed role-playing) societies, plus the ubiquitous community choirs. He cites one study that found Danes are the most sociable nationality. But the other Scandinavian nations are not slouches when it comes to socializing. Swedes are big on volunteer work, Finns love to join community orchestras, outdoor clubs are popular in Norway, and Icelanders have plenty of fraternal organizations and cultural societies.

Scandinavians also have other opportunities to gather, including many holidays around Christmas and Easter time, their equivalents to the US Labor Day, and, of course, midsummer holidays. There are also national holidays, which involve parades and lots of flag-waving, because Scandinavians love their flags. Norwegians also turn out for their Syttende Mai or Norwegian Constitution Day parades and festivities dressed to the nines in their *bunader*, elaborate regional dress. In fact, my introduction to my cousin Anne Berit was a photo of her as a child, marching in her bunad in a Syttende Mai parade in Oslo. (According to Booth, other Scandinavians can be a bit condescending about Norway's all-out, costumed national day celebrations. Although, as he wryly observes, "This from Danes, who . . . will stick their national flag in the cat's litter given the appropriate feline-oriented anniversary."[18])

HYGGE, OF COURSE

Who hasn't heard of hygge by now? Somehow, this Danish version of cozy became an international trend, then a craze. Hygge-induced candle and cocoa sales peaked long ago, yet extra-Nordic hygge has not gone the way of hula hoops and pet rocks. After more than a decade of boutique coziness and selfies of fuzzy socks by roaring fires, hygge is starting to look as perennial as mid-century modern furniture. Yet, it's a custom that, outside Scandinavia, is too often mispronounced, misunderstood, and practiced as a performance art. So, let's dig in and see if we can save hygge.

First, the word. Hygge is thought to come from the old Norse words *hyggja*, meaning "to think," *hygga*, which means "to comfort" (also the origin of the word "hug"), and *hugr*, which means soul, mind, or consciousness. While hygge is often translated as "cozy," a more accurate translation would be a feeling of comfort or satisfaction. While the pronunciation is often simplified for English speakers as "hoo-gah," that's not how Danes say it. The best explanation I've seen is that the "y" is pronounced like "une" in French (similar to German "ü"), and the "e" is pronounced like "ae" in "Michael." If you practice that, you can say it like a Dane if you care to. But Swedes use the word *mys*, and Norwegians say *kos*. Icelanders call it *huggu*, though the term is not as commonly used as in Denmark. The nearest Finnish equivalent (this from many reliable sources) is *kalsarikänni*, or "underpants drunk," which *Travel and Leisure* magazine once described as "the thrilling act of enjoying a good glass of wine in your skivvies."[19] To each his/her own, right?

Despite the recent craze for hygge outside Scandinavia, it is not a new thing. The term has been in use in Denmark since the nineteenth century, and it simply recognizes something that Nordic people have long held dear: enjoying pleasant time together. In fact, hygge is both a noun and a verb. To hygge is to gather and spend time enjoying each other's company, in large groups or small, and letting the cares of the world go for a little while.

This healthy core of coziness in Scandinavian culture is found in meals, celebrations, or just being with others. Some of my own happiest memories are of my family gathering for the evening, listening to music as some of us played games, some read books, and others just dozed in front of the fire. The point was simply to be together, in closeness and comfort. As my old yoga teacher used to say, "We are human beings, not human doings." So perhaps hygge is the Nordic equivalent of emotional yoga. If hygge does stick around in the non-Nordic world, I hope it will come to be practiced more as a way of reaching this peaceful state of mind.

COMMUNITY IN NORDIC ARTS AND CRAFTS

As in most cultures, a lot of historical folk art and craft in Scandinavia was devoted to social purposes, from ceremonial clothing to utensils and textiles. Here are just a few examples of Nordic arts and crafts made for social occasions.

Ale Bowls

Getting together for a beer is an ancient Nordic tradition, going back at least to the Vikings. According to researcher Carol Hasvold, pre-Christian worship included communal drinking of home-brewed ale, in a ceremony called *blote*.[20] Intoxication was thought to open a connection to the gods and bring good luck to the family. After the conversion to Christianity, ale consumption ramped down considerably, but ale was still brewed and consumed for special occasions, including birth, baptism, marriage, and funerals.

Of course, ritual ale required a ritual vessel, and these came in many forms. In Viking through medieval times, ale was usually drunk from a drinking horn, literally a hollowed-out ox or goat horn, sometimes with metal feet so that the horn could be set down without spilling the contents. From the fifteenth century on, ale was more typically served in wooden ale bowls, so that it could be passed around. Over the centuries, the bowls became more ornate, with rosemaling or carved designs. There were oval, boat-shaped ones with horse or dragon heads at each end as handles. There were "ale hens" with heads and tails for handles, although the "hen" head might also be a duck or goose. There were staved ones, like miniature, embellished barrels, and round, turned bowls with lines and, sometimes, painted

Hand-carved large ale bowl with handles carved in the shape of horse's heads with a small man hanging from each bridle. The inscription reads: *Drik om ver from led kjengen blive tom. Jon Endre Sen dalen 1816* (Drink around and be pious, let the bowl be empty. Jon Endre Sen Valley 1816). Jon Enderson Folkedal, Granvin, Hordaland, Norway. Collection of Vesterheim Norwegian-American Museum, Decorah, Iowa.

inscriptions, to give guests a cue about how much they could politely consume before passing the bowl to the next person. As Hasvold observes, while there was excess, the fact that so many ale bowls have survived in beautiful condition shows that ale was more about ritual and community than intoxication.

Skillbragd

The *skillbragd* (Norwegian) or *opphämta* (Swedish) coverlet is one of the most distinctive Scandinavian textiles, and it played an important role in social observances from the seventeenth century up to the early twentieth century. These coverlets are woven with overshot patterning, meaning that the colored pattern yarn floats above a tightly woven, usually neutral-colored ground cloth, which provides both background and structural integrity. Skillbragd requires either a special, time-consuming loom set-up, or the pattern can be picked up by hand, using a weaving sword; the skill and time involved explain why these coverlets were made or given for special occasions.

In *Woven Coverlets of Norway*,[21] Katherine Larson relates that skillbragd coverlets were used as christening blankets throughout Norway and that, when several infants were brought for christening on a Sunday, the locals paid close attention to which child was wrapped in the finest, most colorful coverlet. The mention of overshot coverlets in estate documents suggests that they were precious enough to be figured into a dowry or inheritance. There are also surviving examples of

Detail of skillbragd on
the loom. Photo by John
Capone.

Skillbragd on a loom at
Merit Anny Tvenge
Vevsto, Vestre Slidre
Municipality, Norway.
Photo by John Capone.

Left: Coverlet as it would have been used to drape a coffin. Photo by Anita Osterhaug, taken at Vesterheim Norwegian-American Museum, Decorah, Iowa.

Right: Embroidered symbols on a headdress cloth for a folk costume, pre-1890s, Vossestrand, Voss, Hordeland, Norway. Collection of Vesterheim Norwegian-American Museum, Decorah, Iowa.

skillbragd coverlets with a contrasting square in the center. These would be used to drape a coffin. The square marked the place where a candle was placed, and sometimes the ale bowl before the toast to the dear departed.

My grandmother had two bright, beautiful skillbragd coverlets, one of which may have been a wedding present and one that she carried back with her from a trip to Norway. They're in my home now, and, thanks to the folk art school at the Vesterheim museum, I now know how to weave my own. I will probably never find the time, but it helps me understand why they were so precious and makes me appreciate Grandma's all the more.

Cloth for Protection and Prosperity

Like many cultures, Scandinavia has a long history of ritual textiles for important social occasions. For example, the Vikings hung special tapestries behind the high seat (the place of honor) at the head of their tables, worked with symbols to ensure health and prosperity. According to the scholar Mary B. Kelly,[22] this tradition carried through the nineteenth and into the early twentieth century in remote rural areas. Ceremonial towels embroidered with fertility goddesses and sun symbols were hung behind the bride's and groom's seats at weddings—symbols carried down virtually unchanged from Viking times. Cloths with sun and knot symbols for protection wrapped gifts of food to a new mother and covered a baby at christening. Cloth with fertility symbols such as a ram's horn were given to a bride and groom, and an equal-armed cross, the symbol of transition to other worlds, might be embroidered on a burial cloth.

THE ART OF KAFFE: COZIES FOR A FESTIVE FIKA

by SARAH SHIPPEN

CRAFT: *Knitting*

DIFFICULTY LEVEL: *Intermediate*

Fika is a break for coffee, tea, and sweet pastries, but most of all it is an opportunity for a quick catch-up with family, colleagues, and community. This tea-and-coffee cozy set with matching mug rugs is designed to delight the eye, keep the drinks hot, and make the table look as sweet as the pastries! I took my pattern inspiration from *krokbragd* weaving patterns found on traditional Norwegian coverlets. Their bold colors will brighten up the room, even on long winter days. And, in the Nordic tradition of never wasting anything, the small amounts of yarn used in the patterns will allow you to use your wool stash to make a whole collection of pieces. Knitting these is a breeze, so brighten your own table or knit a set for a gift and give them along with a package of your favorite coffee or tea!

The tea-and-coffee cozies are knitted in the round, like a sweater, and utilize the same multicolor stranded technique. If you're new to Nordic knitting, these small projects will give you experience and confidence to take on the larger challenge of a knitted sweater! They also involve steeks (a section of knitting that is meant to be cut, usually to add armholes or to open a cardigan front). Knitting a small steek is great practice for sweater knitting.

Structure: Stranded knitting

Materials

Yarn Rauma 3-tråds Strikkegarn (100% wool; 118 yd [108 m] / 1.75 oz [50 g]):

>   **MC:** #116 Dark Brown Heather, 1 ball
>
>   **CC1:** #460 Light Beige, 1 ball
>
>   **CC2:** #124 Red, 1 ball
>
>   **CC3:** #177 Dark Orange, 1 ball

1 ball of each color provides enough yarn to knit the tea cozy, cafetière (French press) cover, and mug rugs in this chapter as well as the cup cuffs in chapter 5.

Needles Size 4 (3.5 mm): 24" circular (cir) and set of double-pointed (dpn) or additional 24" cir. For mug rugs only: Sizes 10 (6 mm) and 11 (8 mm): straight. Adjust needle size if necessary to obtain the correct gauge.

Notions Markers (m); locking m; 1–2 yd laceweight wool yarn in contrasting color (optional); size E/4 (3.5 mm) crochet hook for making button loop; tapestry needle.

Gauge 22 sts and 26 rnds = 4" in stranded patt on smallest needle.

Detail of a krokbragd coverlet made by Margerethe Sella or Susan Kjørnes, Norway, ca. 1870–1900. Collection of Vesterheim Norwegian-American Museum, Decorah, Iowa.

These pieces use Rauma 100% wool yarn, a beautiful two-ply DK yarn spun from the glossy wool of Norwegian sheep. There is a large range of beautiful colors, and it fulls beautifully during washing and blocking to a smooth and lovely finished hand.

Dimensions

Finished Size: Tea cozy is sized for a teapot with 20¼" circumference at the widest point, and it can stretch to fit a 23" teapot. The finished cozy is 7½" tall. From cast-on edge to handle opening is ¾". Opening for the handle and spout is 3¾" high.

Cafetière cover is sized for a French press with 12" circumference. The cozy is about 5½" tall.

Mug rugs are 4¼" square after fulling.

You can easily adapt these pieces to the size of your teapot or coffeepot. The steek height can be adjusted as needed for different handles. And to make the circumference larger or smaller, just add or remove stitches as necessary at the end of the pattern and before the steek. The steek opening will keep any issues with pattern repeats from being a problem.

Notes

- The cozies are worked in the round from the bottom up with steeks. The mug rugs are worked back and forth in rows.
- When working stranded knitting, be consistent with which color is knitted from above and which from below the carried yarn. For best color definition, knit pattern colors from below (or hold in left hand) and background colors from above (or hold in right hand).
- Three colors are used on Round 33 of each cozy. You can work with three colors on that round, or you can add the third color by working duplicate stitch during finishing.
- The pieces are washed and lightly fulled. Fulling also serves to secure stitches for the steek and give the piece a little more structure. Handwash each piece in warm water with mild soap, squeezing and agitating to produce some fulling. Don't be too gentle, this wool can handle it!

Stitch Guide

Alternating-color cable cast-on (ACCO): With MC, place a lark's head knot on left needle with bar at back and tail on left. (See below for lark's head knot instructions.)

Insert right needle between legs of knot (see photo **1**) and wrap CC1 as if to knit (see photo **2**). Pull CC1 through, then transfer this st onto left needle as if to knit (see photo **3**).

*Insert right needle between last 2 sts on left needle. Pick up MC from behind, pulling it forward (see photo **4**), then wrap it around right needle as if to knit, pull new st through, and transfer st to left needle as if to knit.

Rep from * until there is 1 more st on needle than needed. Working yarns will twist as you proceed, so periodically suspend your work by holding both yarns and letting them untwist. Before joining work in the rnd, drop first MC st (left leg of lark's head knot).

Backward loop cast-on (BLCO): Make a slipknot about 3" from end of yarn and place on needle.

Holding needle in right hand, *bring yarn from needle behind tip of left index finger, and rotate finger to your right to make a loop around finger. With needle, pick up loop on finger from below, then tighten on needle. Rep from * for desired numbers of sts.

Linen stitch (LS) (odd number of sts): Note: Always wrap working yarn around selvage at end of row.

Row 1 (RS): K1, *sl 1 pwise wyf, k1; rep from * to end.

Row 2 (WS): Sl 1 pwise wyb, *p1, sl 1 pwise wyb; rep from * to end.

Rep Rows 1 and 2 for patt.

Lark's head knot: Fold yarn a few inches from end and hold the ends in your right hand. Put your left index finger and thumb through the folded loop, reach outward, and pick up both sides of the yarn below the loop from the outside. Pinch yarns together,

1. Insert needle between legs of lark's head knot and pick up a stitch of CC1.

2. Place new stitch back on left needle.

3. Insert needle between last 2 stitches and pick up a stitch of MC.

4. Repeat until you have desired number of stitches plus 1, ending with CC1.

and bring the bar of the loop down in front of the pinched yarn. Your fingers are now holding the lark's head knot, and you can slip it onto a needle with the loop bar in front or back. (Page 170, photo 1, shows a lark's head knot.)

Blanket stitch: Fold steek to inside of fabric. Using a coordinating yarn and tapestry needle, catch stitch on back of fabric and bring needle up through steek about ¼" from edge. *Bring yarn to the right and hold with left hand, then bring yarn up and away from you, making a reverse "L" on top of the steek. Bring needle behind the steek, catch the back of the main fabric, then sew up through the steek at the bend of the reverse "L." Repeat from *, moving to the right, until you have sewn down the whole steek. On the last stitch, pass the needle back under the "L" of the stitch and knot the yarn under the steek. (Also see www.wikihow.com/Sew-Blanket-Stitch for step-by-step videos.)

Working Steeks

The knitting charts show 7-stitch steeks. The steeks are worked in a checkerboard of alternating colors (as shown on the charts). This ensures that the yarns will full together during finishing and prevent the cut edge from raveling.

Use the backward loop cast-on method and the working yarns to add the steek stitches in colors as shown on the chart. (The yarn is attached, so you won't need to begin with a slip-knot.) These stitches will be folded back and hidden when finished.

When the steek area is completed, bind off the steek stitches and pull the working stitches together by folding the steek.

When the item is complete, weave in ends and full the piece (see Notes).

Once fulled, there is very little chance of the cut edge raveling, but if you choose, you can quickly secure these stitches with a running stitch, using a darning needle and some laceweight yarn.

Cut open the steek along the center of the middle stitch (at the bottom of the "vee" of the knit stitch).

Turn the steek flaps inside the piece, using the MC column of stitches as the folding point, and sew the flaps to the inside.

Try the piece on the cafetière or teapot and decide how long an opening you'll need for your pot. If it is too long, use an invisible stitch to shorten the opening as needed.

Here are two guides you may find helpful:
- The Twisted Yarn's "How to Steek" tutorial: www.thetwistedyarn.com/2014/08/14/tutorial-how-to-steek
- KnittingHelp.com's "Backward Loop Cast-on": www.youtube.com/watch?v=btn5UwTfY-k

Tea Cozy Instructions

With smallest cir needle and using the Alternating-Color Cable method (see Stitch Guide), CO 112 sts, ending with CC1. Break CC1, leaving a 6" tail.

Working back and forth in rows, knit 2 rows.

Transfer sts to dpn or 2 cir needles, place marker (pm), and join in the rnd.

Working in St st, work Rnds 1–3 of Tea Cozy Color chart.

Next rnd (Rnd 4 of chart): Work 56 sts in patt, pm, using the backward-loop method, CO 7 sts for steek using colors as shown on chart, pm, work in patt to end, pm, then CO 7 sts for steek using colors as shown on chart—126 sts: 112 cozy sts and 14 steek sts.

Cont in patt through Rnd 28 of chart—112 sts rem: 98 cozy sts and 14 steek sts.

Next rnd (Rnd 29 of chart): *Work in patt to steek m, then, using alternating colors, BO 7 steek sts; rep from * once more—84 sts rem.

On next rnd, fold each steek to pull sts tog as best you can.

Work in patt through Rnd 46 of chart, working Rnds 35, 39, 43, and 45 as foll:

Rnds 35, 39, 43, and 45: Work in patt to last st, k2tog (removing m), pm for new beg of rnd.

14 sts rem when chart is complete.

Next rnd: With CC2, [k2tog] 7 times—7 sts rem.

Break yarn, leaving a 12" tail. Thread tail onto tapestry needle and draw through rem sts. Pull tight to gather sts and fasten off on WS.

Finishing

Weave in ends. Full piece (see Notes). Allow piece to dry until just barely damp. Cut steek while piece is still damp, fold flaps to WS, and put cozy on teapot

Figure 1. Tea Cozy Color Chart

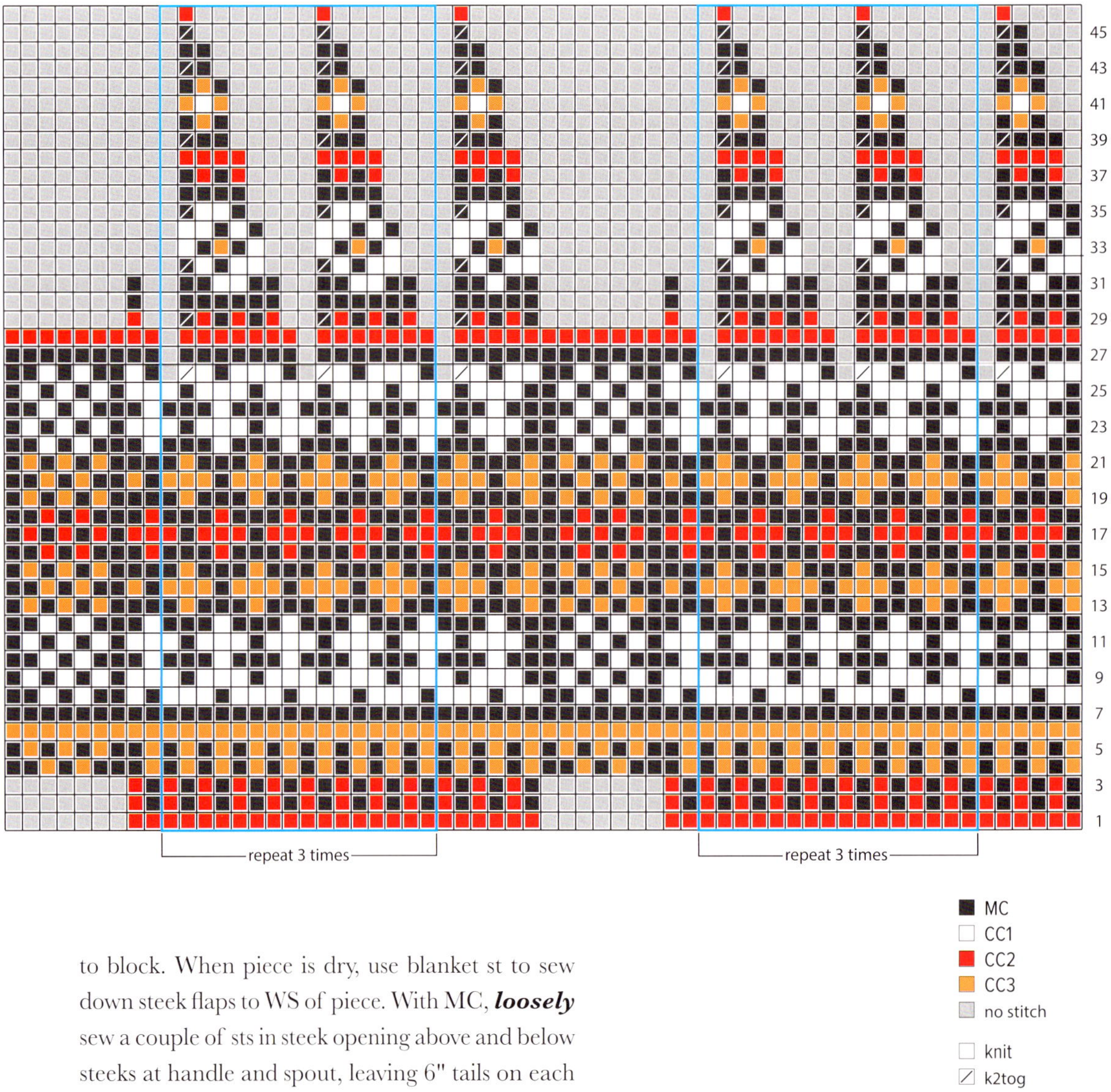

45
43
41
39
37
35
33
31
29
27
25
23
21
19
17
15
13
11
9
7
5
3
1

└─────repeat 3 times─────┘   └─────repeat 3 times─────┘

■ MC
□ CC1
■ CC2
■ CC3
■ no stitch

□ knit
◿ k2tog

to block. When piece is dry, use blanket st to sew down steek flaps to WS of piece. With MC, *loosely* sew a couple of sts in steek opening above and below steeks at handle and spout, leaving 6" tails on each set of sts. Put cozy back on pot and gradually pull on these ends to fit your pot. Add or remove sts as needed to get the proper fit. When handle and spout openings are correct length, fasten, tighten, then weave in ends inside cozy.

Optional top loop: With crochet hook and MC, make a slipknot, leaving a 6" tail and ch 13. Fasten off, leaving a 6" tail. Thread each tail on a tapestry needle, sew from RS through center top and secure inside cozy.

Cafetière Cozy Instructions

With smallest cir needle and using the Alternating-Color Cable method (see Stitch Guide), CO 66 sts, ending with CC1. Break CC1, leaving a 6" tail.

Working back and forth in rows, knit 2 rows.

Work Row 1 of Cafetière Cozy Color chart to last 7 sts of chart.

Transfer sts to dpn or 2 cir needles.

At end of Row 1, pm, using the backward-loop method (see Stitch Guide), CO 7 sts for steek—73 sts: 66 cozy sts and 7 steek sts.

Cont in patt through Rnd 37 of chart.

Next rnd (Rnd 38 of chart): Work in patt to steek m, then BO 7 steek sts— 66 sts rem.

On next rnd, fold steek and pull body sts tog.

Work in patt through Rnd 40 of chart.

BO all sts, alternating MC and CC1 as established on Rnd 40, making sure that BO is loose enough to maintain gauge of last rnd.

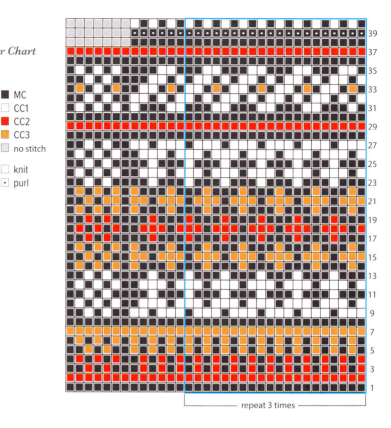

Figure 2. Cafetière Cozy Color Chart

■ MC
□ CC1
■ CC2 (red)
■ CC3 (orange)
▨ no stitch

□ knit
⊡ purl

repeat 3 times

Finishing

Weave in ends. Full piece (see Notes). Allow piece to dry until just barely damp. Cut steek while piece is still damp, fold flaps to WS, and put cozy on coffee pot to block. When piece is dry, use blanket st to sew down steek flaps to WS of piece.

Knitted button: With MC, smallest needle, and using the long-tail method, leaving an 8" tail, CO 15 sts. BO all sts. Break yarn, leaving an 8" tail. Stretch and, beg at one end of piece, tightly roll into a flat cylinder (like a cinnamon roll). Keeping piece tightly rolled, thread the 8" tail on outside of roll onto a tapestry needle and sew from outside of button through middle and out opposite side to secure sts. Rep 4 to 5 times, moving around outside and going through center until button is firmly secure. Sew into button once more and come out at bottom next to other tail.

Place cozy onto cafetière and pull sides tog below handle. Find best place for button, mark with a locking m, remove cozy, and sew button onto cafetière using the two tails.

Button loop: With crochet hook and MC, make a slipknot, leaving an 8" tail. Ch 11. Fasten off, leaving an 8" tail. With cozy on cafetière, place button loop around button and determine best location for both ends of loop. Mark end locations with a locking m, remove cozy, and sew on button loop.

If necessary, use MC and tapestry needle to close up and reinforce sts above steek so cozy fits easily, but not too loosely, over handle.

Mug Rug Instructions

Yarn is doubled for all colors. Mug rugs are worked flat in linen stitch over an odd number of stitches.

With middle-size needle, 2 strands each of MC and CC1, and using the Alternating-Color Cable method (see Stitch Guide), CO 15 sts, ending with MC. Break CC1, leaving a 6" tail.

Work in linen st (see Stitch Guide) for 26 rows, foll Mug Rug Color chart. Break yarn. Change to largest needle.

Next row (RS): With 2 strands of CC1 held tog, leaving a 6" tail, work in linen st.

Break yarn, leaving a 6" tail.

Next row (WS): With 2 strands of MC held tog, leaving a 6" tail, work in linen st.

Break yarn, leaving a 6" tail. (The tails from these rows will be knotted during finishing.)

BO without knitting sts as foll: With RS facing and middle-size needle, sl 1 pwise, *sl 1 pwise, pass 2nd st over first; rep from * to end. Fasten off.

Finishing

Tie MC and CC1 tails tog at each end of CO with overhand knot. Rep for BO end. If both colors are not included at the end, add a short length of missing color and tie overhand knot. Trim ends to about 1". Weave in rem ends. Place mug rugs in a basin of warm, soapy water and agitate vigorously to full. Rinse and roll in towel to remove water. Flatten each rug and gently pull to 4¼" square, then set aside to dry. When dry, trim corner knots to about ½".

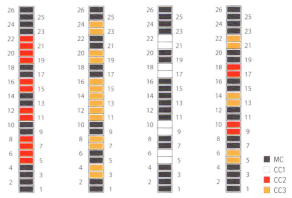

Figure 3. Mug Rug Color Chart

Tips for Working Linen Stitch

- Color changes happen only when starting the right side (knit-facing) rows.
- Always wrap working yarn around edge of piece to create smooth edges.
- The floats from the slipped stitches are always on the right (knit-facing) side.
- The right-side (knit-facing) rows always begin and end with a k1.
- The wrong-side (purl-facing) rows always begin and end with a sl 1.

PICK-ME-UP NAPKINS

by ELISABETH HILL

CRAFT: *Weaving*

DIFFICULTY LEVEL: *Advanced beginner*

These napkins were inspired by an upholstery fabric in Swedish weaver Malin Selander's endlessly fascinating book *Weaving Patterns*, published in 1956 (Göteborg, Sweden: Wezäta Förlag). She calls this fabric "Check Upholstery with Weft Skips" or Morrhoppen. The design, though over fifty years old, looks modern and graphic—the timelessness of mid-century modern design. I adapted it for the rigid-heddle loom, using a simple pick-up pattern. My design allows variations in the color, and you can also vary the design repeats. So, you can weave a matching set of napkins without falling into the "second sock" syndrome, the boredom that can keep a project on your needles or loom for far too long.

Despite Scandinavian practicality, Malin Selander could also be a renegade about floats in weaving. According to one story, she was wearing a gorgeous handwoven top at an American weaving conference. The top had sleeves that were mostly unwoven warp threads, and when someone asked how she washed a fabric that was so fragile, without missing a beat she replied, "I don't." Unlike Malin's lovely blouse, these table linens will wash very nicely.

Structure: Plain weave with supplementary weft floats

Equipment

Rigid-heddle loom, 20" weaving width; 12-dent reed; 3 or 4 stick shuttles; 1 pick-up stick.

Materials

Yarns

Warp: 22/2 cottolin (3,200 yd/lb; Bockens), #2072 Cream, 680 yd; #2073 Almond, 680 yd; #2047 Sienna, 168 yd.

Weft: 22/2 cottolin, #2072 Cream and #2073 Almond, 560 yd each; #2047 Sienna, 187yd; #2012 Dandelion, #2011 Yellow Ochre, and #2062 Apple, 80 yd each.

Note: All yarns are used doubled except for the Cream weft on the inner hems. Almond and Cream are used together, 1 strand of each, for the warp and the plain-weave weft.

Other supplies: Sewing thread to match the Almond/Cream cottolin.

Warp Length

218 working ends 3½ yd (126") long (allows 9" for take-up, 33" for sampling and loom waste).

Setts

Warp: 12 epi.

Weft: 12 ppi; 24 ppi in pick-up areas.

Dimensions

Width in the heddle: $18^2/_{12}$".

Woven length: (measured under tension on the loom) 84".

Finished size: (after wet-finishing and hemming) Four napkins, $15^1/_2$" by 16".

Instructions

1. Set up your loom for direct warping a length of 126" or wind a warp of 218 ends 126" long, following the warp color order in figure 1. Remember that the Sienna is used doubled, and the light warp ends are one thread each of Cream and Almond. Warp the loom using your preferred method, centering for a weaving width of $18^2/_{12}$" and making sure that your first warp end on the right is in a hole (not a slot).

2. Wind one stick shuttle with 1 strand of Cream, to use for the inner hems. Wind another with 2 strands of Sienna, and the last one with 1 strand each of Cream and Almond.

3. Spread the warp with scrap yarn.

4. Weave 8 picks of the Cream for the inner hems. (This thinner fabric will make it easier to turn the hem under neatly.) Then weave 30 picks with Almond/Cream, ending on a up shed.

5. With the heddle in a neutral position, working behind the heddle and starting 20 ends from the right selvedge, use your pick-up stick to pick up the following sequence:

Under 1 (this end should be in a hole), over 5
Under 2, over 2, under 2, over 6, under 6, over 2, under 6, over 6 (repeat ** 5 x)
Under 2, over 2, under 2, over 5, under 1

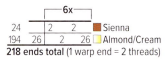

Figure 1. Warp Color Order

	6x			
24	2	2		■ Sienna
194	26	2	26	□ Almond/Cream

218 ends total (1 warp end = 2 threads)

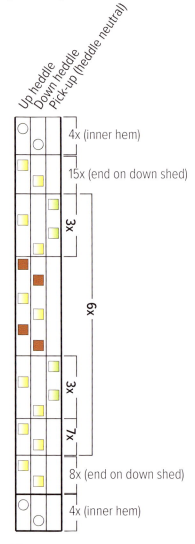

Figure 2. Weft Color Order

Up heddle
Down heddle
Pick-up (heddle neutral)

4x (inner hem)
15x (end on down shed)
3x
6x
3x
7x
8x (end on down shed)
4x (inner hem)

■ Sienna
□ Almond/Cream
□ inlay color
(Sienna, Dandelion, Yellow Ochre, or Apple)

Weaving Tips

- The pick-up shed is narrow, and it takes a little practice to get the weft through it without skips. Be patient, and it will come. It helps if you can use a thinner shuttle and don't overload it with yarn.
- The up/down order is important in this project for catching the supplemental weft. Pay attention and follow the weaving order!

6. Turn the pick-up stick on its side behind the heddle and weave a pick with the Sienna weft. Turn the pick-up stick flat, push it to the back of the loom, and weave an up pick with Almond/ Cream. Bring the pick-up stick forward with the heddle in neutral, weave another pick with Sienna, flatten the pick-up stick and push it to the back, then weave a down pick with Almond/Cream. (The Sienna inlay doesn't not go all the way to the selvedges, so the design will include a small line where it changes directions between picks.) Repeat this sequence three times, as shown in figure 2.

7. Continue weaving the first napkin, following the weaving order shown in figure 2. After the inlay sections, end with 30 picks of Almond/Cream, the 8 picks of Cream for inner hem.

8. Weave in 1 or 2 picks of a contrasting yarn, wind the fourth stick shuttle with double strands of Dandelion, Apple, or Yellow Ochre, and weave the next napkin, using Sienna for the plain-weave stripes and the other color for the inlay. Continue weaving the additional napkins, separating them with a few contrasting picks and changing inlay color for each one.

9. Remove your fabric from the loom and zigzag or serge the raw ends.

10. Machine-wash the fabric in warm water with mild soap, then tumble dry.

11. Cut the napkins apart. Turn the inner hem under, then turn the hem under again and iron. Sew hems by hand or machine.

12. Iron and voilà! Ready to use. (There is no Scandinavian word for *voilà*, to my knowledge.)

RUSTIC LINEN PLACE MATS

by ANITA OSTERHAUG

CRAFT: *Weaving*

DIFFICULTY LEVEL: *Advanced beginner*

These place mats are inspired by the contemporary, minimalist Scandinavian aesthetic, but they show off the beauty of linen just as well as the fine linen fabrics that graced my grandmother's table. The colors of the cottolin warp, chosen to match Lisa Hill's napkins, interact with the coarse yet shining linen weft to create pretty color variations in the squares. Like all linen, these place mats will soften with time and washing, becoming even more pleasurable to use.

A note on the warping: I wove these on a Glimakra Siru rigid-heddle loom from Sweden. The heddle I used is sold as twelve-dent (twelve slots/holes per inch), but it's actually metric and closer to a 13-dent. If you have a different loom and you want to weave place mats the same size as mine, you can drop two warp threads from each brown, green, and gold warp stripe for a twelve-dent heddle, or drop one thread from each of those stripes for a 12.5-dent heddle.

Structure: Plain weave

Equipment
Rigid-heddle loom, 15" weaving width; 13-dent heddle (see note above); 2 stick shuttles; thin-edged pick-up stick or weaving sword; 2 large S-hooks or other weights for selvedge bundles; a pair of small, sharp scissors; small crochet hook; tapestry needle.

Materials
Yarns

Warp: 22/2 cottolin (3,200 yd/lb; Bockens), #2072 Cream, 84 yd; #2047 Sienna, 224 yd, #2062 Apple and #2050 Golden Orange (or substitute #2012 Dandelion), 208 yd each.

Weft: Mattlin 4/6 (100% flax; 200 yd/lb, 218 yd/17.6 oz cone; Bockens), #6300 Rust, 88 yd; #1095 Lime Green and #1001 Ochre, 52 yd each; #1003 Half Bleached, 38 yd.

Warp Length

183 ends 4 yd (144") long (includes tripled floating selvedges; allows 10" for take-up, 31" for loom waste and sampling; loom waste includes fringe).

Setts

Warp: 13 epi. (Your epi may be different, depending on your rigid heddle.)

Weft: About 8 ppi.

Dimensions

Width in the heddle: $13^8/_{13}$" in a 13-dent heddle plus extra width to turn the linen weft at the selvedges.

Woven length: (measured under tension on the loom) 103".

Finished size: Four place mats, 14" by 17".

Figure 1. Warp Color Order

21		21		☐ Cream
52		26	26	🟧 Golden Orange
52		26	26	🟩 Apple
52	26		26	🟥 Sienna

177 ends total (does not include extra selvedge threads)

Figure 2. Weft Color Order

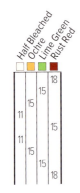

Numbers indicate picks of that color.

Instructions

1. Set up your loom for direct warping a length of 144" or wind a warp of 177 ends 4 yd long, following the warp color order in figure 1. (Or adjust number of ends to your rigid heddle.) Measure 4 extra ends of the Sienna and set aside for the selvedges. Warp the loom using your preferred method, centering for a weaving width of $13^8/_{13}$" and making sure that your first warp and last ends are in holes. Before you tie the warp to the back apron rod, thread 2 more ends of Sienna together through the holes on either side of the warp, to triple the selvedges, then tie on. Once the loom is warped, hang a large S-hook or other weight over each selvedge bundle to keep them taught. (Fishing weights hung on paper clips work fine, too.)

2. Spread the warp with scrap yarn, allowing at least 6" for fringe. If you like, weave an inch or two with Mattlin to practice turning the yarn around the selvedge and keeping the selvedges even. You can pull these picks out later, along with the scrap yarn. Finish by weaving 1" more with scrap yarn.

3. Wind linen yarn on the stick shuttle for the first weft stripe. (Refer to figure 2, the weft color order, for the number of picks in each stripe.) The flax weft yarn is heavy, and you also won't want to waste it, so measure out just enough for each stripe before winding it on a stick shuttle. The first stripe has 18 picks, so measure out a length of the Rust Mattlin that is 19 times the width of your warp, then cut the weft yarn and wind it onto your stick shuttle. The extra length is for tails to weave in, and gives a little extra weft to bend around the warp at the selvedges.

4. Begin to weave the first stripe, leaving about a 5" tail at the selvedge. Push the pick into place with the rigid heddle. Then open the shed again, split the plies of the tail, bend half of the threads around the tripled selvedge, and tuck them into the shed with your first pick. With the crochet hook, catch one of the tail threads and pull it out toward you about 2" from the selvedge. Pull another out toward you an inch or so further from the selvedge. (See photo **1**.) You'll clip these off later, when you're finishing the place mats. Weave the next pick, then tuck the remaining tail threads into that shed and pull two out to taper as before. Push that pick into place with the rigid-heddle. When you open the shed for the next pick, use the pick-up stick or weaving sword to really snug the previous pick into place, then weave the next pick.

5. Weave the remaining 16 picks of this stripe, using the weaving sword to push each pick firmly into place. (See photo **2**.) As you weave, pay attention and make sure to keep the edges even as you bend the flax around the selvedge. As you complete the last pick, leave a 5" tail and split the plies as you did before. Bend half the plies around the selvedge, tuck them in with the last pick, and bring a couple plies forward as before to taper.

6. Measure enough Lime Green weft for the next stripe and wind onto the stick shuttle. Open the shed for the next pick, tuck the 3 remaining tail threads from the last Rust pick into this shed, and taper as before. Lay the Lime Green into the shed, leaving about a 5" tail at the selvedge. Pull a thread out at each place where a Rust thread ends, so that you have only 6 threads at any point in the shed. Change sheds, pack in this pick, tuck in and taper the remaining 3 threads of the Lime Green tail into the next pick as before. (See photo **3**.)

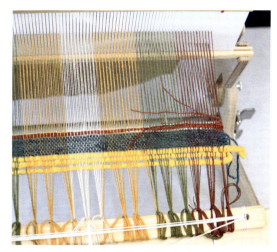

1. Tucking in tail of the first weft pick.

2. Packing down the weft with the sharp-edged pick-up stick.

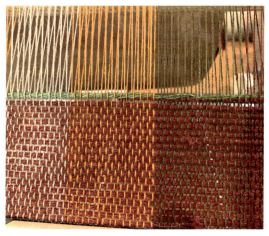

3. Tucking in ends at a color change.

7. Continue weaving in this way, following the weft color order in figure 2, ending each stripe by tucking in its tail, then beginning the next stripe from the opposite side of the warp. At the end of the last stripe, tuck and taper half the tail into the last shed, then use the tapestry needle to work the remaining plies into the previous shed, tapering them as usual.

8. Weave an inch or so of scrap yarn, skip about 5" of warp for fringe allowance, weave another inch with scrap yarn, then weave the second place mat as you did the first. (If you prefer, you can weave in some old window blind slats or ten $\frac{1}{2}$" wide strips of cardboard between the place mats to keep the 5" of warp free. Either way works, but the slats or cardboard can give you a straight line to begin weaving against for the next place mat.) Weave the third and fourth place mats, weaving 1" scrap yarn before and after each one and leaving an additional 5" of warp free between the place mats for fringe.

9. Remove your fabric from the loom, leaving at least 5" of warp at the end for fringes.

10. Cut the place mats apart at the midpoint of the free warp between them.

11. One place mat and one end at a time, pull about 10 warp ends free from the scrap yarn, snug them down against the place mat end, and tie them tightly in an overhand knot up against the edge. The number of threads in your bundles may vary, depending on how many warp ends you used with your rigid heddle. Mine have 9 or 10 threads in each and there are 17 fringe bundles. Cut the fringe bundles about $\frac{3}{4}$" from the knot. (I just grasped them between my thumb and forefinger and used the width of my thumb as a guide.)

12. When the fringe is finished, take your small scissors and snip off all the tail threads sticking out of the place mats.

13. There is no need to wet-finish these place mats before you use them. When you do need to wash them, I suggest washing on a gentle cycle in warm water, then hanging to dry. If the flax is stiff, you can shake them a few times or tumble dry briefly to soften them up again. If the tip of a tail thread works its way out with use, you can snip it off or leave it and just enjoy the rustic nature of this beautiful flax.

Weaving and Other Tips

- Use a fuzzy wool for the scrap yarn spacers. I used Lett Lopi Icelandic yarn that was left over from another project. It stayed in place well when the place mats came off the loom, keeping the warp threads organized until I was ready to tie the fringe.

- In this project, there is a lot of warp take-up. (A lot of warp length is needed to go over and under the weft yarns.) To allow for this, advance your warp often, and try to keep a consistent warp tension, and not too tight. The warp threads need to be able to relax around the weft once the place mats are off the loom, and even tension will give you a good, firm weave and consistent lengths among the place mats.

- Do use a weaving sword or pick-up stick to snug each pick in place before making the next one. With this thick, stiff weft, it's hard to get enough pressure with the rigid-heddle alone.

- It is really important to have enough weight on the selvedge warp bundles as you weave. All the other warp threads weave over and under the thick weft threads. But the selvedge bundles don't travel over and under: the weft threads bend around them instead. The weights compensate for this difference in take-up, keeping the selvedges under the same tension as the rest of the warp.

- The Mattlin flax weft in this is stiff and strong, so it resists turning around the tripled selvedge. You'll also notice that it pushes the three warp ends closest to the selvedge and causes them to squish together. Let it happen. It makes for a sturdy, attractive edge.

- Pay close attention to keeping the selvedge loops even. To keep a constant width, measure often, and use a weaving temple if you have one. Because it is stiff, the Mattlin will bend in wide loops at first. As it relaxes and as more picks are pressing on it, those loops will squish down and become longer.

- If you find that the weft tails are stacking up at one side of the place mat, you can choose to start each weft stripe at the opposite edge from where the last stripe ended. If you do this, taper the tail of the color that's ending and split it between the last pick of that color and the first pick of the new color. Taper the tail of the new color at the selvedge and split it between the first and second picks of that color.

MONK'S BELT TOWELS OF WELCOME

by ANITA OSTERHAUG

CRAFT: *Weaving*

DIFFICULTY LEVEL: *Advanced beginner*

By my grandmother's generation, Scandinavians no longer looked to embroidered linens for magical protection. But the women of my family would never have invited company without putting out a pretty linen hand towel in the bathroom, and Grandma embroidered many a dainty towel for her granddaughters' future homes. Instead of embroidery, these little towels are patterned with monk's belt, a simple block pattern that's common in traditional Scandinavian coverlets. They're made with cottolin thread, which is a bit more absorbent and easier to launder than pure linen.

The cottolin yarn is used doubled in the warp and weft, and in the monk's belt pick-up patterning the colored yarn is used tripled. Cottolin comes in a whole range of luscious colors. So, if you like these, weave more in colors for every occasion and season. They also make pretty hostess, holiday, or wedding gifts.

Structure: Plain weave with monk's belt

Equipment

Rigid-heddle loom, 17" weaving width; 10-dent reed; 2 or 3 stick shuttles; pick-up stick; tapestry needle for weaving in ends.

Materials

Yarns

Warp: 22/2 cottolin (3,200 yd/lb; Bockens; Glimakra USA), #2000 Half Bleached, 648 yd.

Weft: 22/2 cottolin, #2000 Half Bleached, 610 yd; #2032 Light Turquoise and #2059 Darkest Turquoise, 60 yd each.

Warp Length

162 ends 2 yd (72") long (warp yarn is used doubled; allows 5" for take-up, 23" for loom waste).

Setts

Warp: 10 epi.

Weft: About 14 ppi; 28 ppi in inlay areas.

Dimensions

Width in the reed: $16\frac{2}{10}$" in a 10-dent reed.

Woven length: (measured under tension on the loom) 44".

Finished size: (after wet-finishing and hemming) Two towels, 14" by 20".

Instructions

1. Set up your loom for direct warping a length of 72" or wind a warp of 162 ends 2 yd long. Remember that the cottolin is used doubled. If you have two spools of the white (half bleached) cottolin, you can warp from both spools at the same time. If you only have one, wind two balls that you can work from while warping. As you warp, use your fingers to maintain even tension on the two threads. Warp the loom, centering for a weaving width of $16\,^2/_{10}$".

2. Spread the warp with scrap yarn. I suggest using something woolen and a little fuzzy, such as scraps of Lopi. This will stay in place to protect the end once you have the fabric off the loom.

3. Wind a stick shuttle with about 10 yd of single white cottolin and weave $^3/_4$" in plain weave. This will be turned under for the hem.

4. Wind a stick shuttle with doubled white cottolin and another with tripled cottolin in either of the pattern colors. Again, this will be easiest if you wind balls of the yarn and then wind the balls together onto the stick shuttle, using your fingers to maintain even tension on the strands.

5. Weave 2" in plain weave with the Half Bleached on the stick shuttle for the first weft stripe, then weave the pick-up pattern as shown in figure 1. Alternate monk's belt pattern picks with plain-weave picks of the white weft. Notice that the monk's belt pattern picks don't go all the way to the edge of the cloth. They turn two warp ends from the edge, making a little turning line on the back of the towel.

Old monk's belt fabric, Nordiska Museet, Stockholm, Sweden. Photo by Veronna Capone.

6. When the monk's belt pattern is complete, weave in plain-weave with white until the piece measures 18" from the beginning. Wind a stick shuttle with about 10 yds of doubled yarn in the pattern color. Weave 3 plain-weave picks with the pattern color, then three picks with the white weft. Repeat this 6-pick sequence two more times, then finish with three more picks in the pattern color.

7. Weave 2" more with the white weft, then weave $^3/_4$" with single white cottolin as you did at the beginning.

8. Weave a few picks with scrap yarn, then weave the second towel as you did the first, using the other pattern color. Finish with a few more picks of scrap yarn to protect the end.

9. Cut the fabric from the loom, leaving the scrap yarn in place to protect the ends.

10. Machine wash the fabric in warm water, dry, and press with iron on the cotton setting.

11. Fold the ends under about $^1/_4$", iron, then fold under $^1/_2$" again, iron, and handsew hems to the back side (the side where you can see the pattern thread turn).

12. Iron towels, right side down, on top of a fluffy towel to help the pattern threads stand out.

Figure 1. Pick-up Pattern

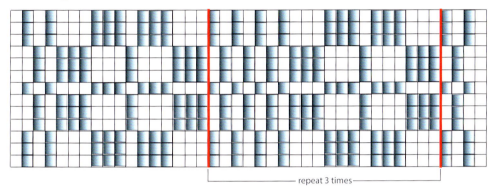

————repeat 3 times————

☐ pick up warp threads

◼ leave warp threads down to be covered by pattern weft

Each square represents 2 doubled warp ends and 2 or 3 picks of the pattern weft.
For the tall columns (3 squares), I wove 8 picks, and I wove 3 picks for the line of single squares in the center. If your beat is firmer, you may want to weave 9 picks for the tall columns and 3 for the squares. Keep in mind that their length will shrink a little when the cloth is no longer under tension on the loom.

Figure 2. Weft Color Order

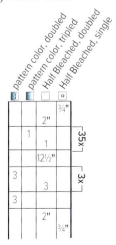

Numbers indicate picks of that color unless followed by the inch symbol ("). In that case, weave that color for as many inches as indicated.

Pick-Up Sequence for the Monk's Belt Pattern

1. With the heddle in a neutral position, pick up warp ends, following the chart and picking up the ends corresponding to the white squares. Each square across represents one pair of doubled warp ends. (See photo **1**.) The warp ends left down will be covered by the pattern weft. Count extra carefully on the first row. After this, it will be easier to see where to pick up.

2. When you finish picking up, turn the pick-up stick on its side and weave a pick through that shed with the pattern weft. (See photos **2** and **3**.) The weft won't come all the way to the selvedge.

3. Turn the pick-up stick flat, remove it, and beat the pick into place.

4. Switch to the next plain-weave shed (heddle in the up or down position) and weave a pick with the white weft, being careful to leave the pattern weft at the back of the cloth. In other words, don't catch it with the white weft.

5. Continue alternating pattern and plain-weave picks as shown in the chart. As noted, the number of picks for each square in the chart will depend on your beat. Weave 8 or 9 picks for the columns (3 squares) and 3 picks for the line of single squares in the center.

1. Picking up the monk's belt pattern.

2. Turn the pick-up stick on its edge to make a shed.

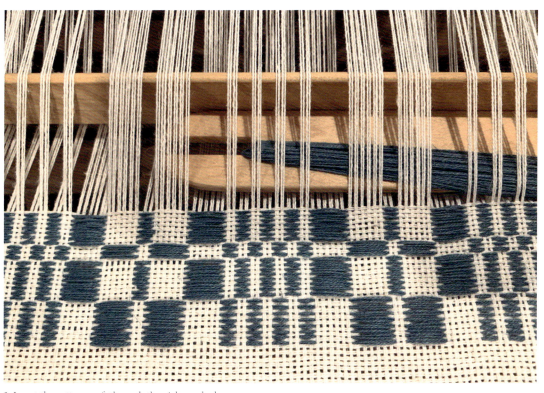

3. Insert the pattern weft through the pick-up shed.

A SWEET AND SIMPLE RUNNER

by SARA BIXLER

CRAFT: *Weaving*

DIFFICULTY LEVEL: *Advanced beginner*

For centuries, Scandinavian householders have loved to welcome guests with lacy linens, from Hardanger embroidery to tatted or woven lace. This sweet runner, with its pretty accents of leno lace, is just the thing to grace a contemporary table. You can weave it as shown here or substitute colors to match your tableware.

Structure: Plain weave with leno

Equipment

Rigid-heddle loom, 14" weaving width; two 10-dent heddles; 3 stick shuttles; pick-up stick, at least 17" long.

Materials

Yarns

Warp: 8/2 cottolin (1,680 yd/8 oz tube; Brassard), #C100 Natural, 400 yd; #C1425 Marine and #C3161 Jaune Or, 80 yd each.

Weft: 8/2 cottolin (1,680 yd/8 oz tube; Brassard), #C100 Natural, 300 yd; #C1425 Marine, 21 yd, #C3161 Jaune Or,1 yd.

Warp Length

280 ends 2 yd (72") long (allows 4" for take-up, 28" for loom waste).

Setts

Warp: 20 epi (using two 10-dent heddles).

Weft: 20 ppi in plain-weave sections; about 10 epi in leno stripes.

Dimensions

Width in the heddle: 14".

Woven length: (measured under tension on the loom) 40".

Finished size: (after wet-finishing and hemming) 12" by 33".

Instructions

1. Set up your loom for direct warping a length of 72" or wind a warp of 280 ends 2 yd long, following the warp color order in figure 1 and warping with the two heddles as shown in figure 2. Warp the loom using your preferred method, centering for a weaving width of 14".

2. Wind stick shuttles with the three weft colors.

3. Spread the warp with a scrap yarn (one that won't run in hot water), then begin the runner by weaving 4¹⁄₂" of plain weave with Natural. Weave the first leno lace sequence as described in the inset, using the Marine weft. Weave 10 picks of plain weave with the Natural, repeat the leno sequence with the Jaune Or weft, weave 10 picks of plain weave with Natural, then repeat the leno sequence once more with the Marine weft.

4. When you finish the leno stripe sequence, weave 24" of plain weave using the Natural. Weave the leno stripe sequence again, then finish by weaving another 4¹⁄₂" of plain weave with Natural. Weave a few picks of plain weave with scrap yarn to protect the end.

5. Cut the fabric from the loom, leaving the scrap yarn in place to protect the ends.

6. Machine wash in warm water, dry, and press with iron on the cotton setting.

7. Fold the ends in about ¹⁄₂", iron, then fold again and handsew hems.

8. Iron finished runner and enjoy!

Weaving with Two Rigid Heddles

In this project, we use two rigid heddles simply to get a finer sett (warp ends per inch) than we could with a single heddle. Weaving plain-weave cloth with two rigid heddles is simple: place both heddles at the same time in either the Up position or the Down position. These positions give you a plain-weave shed; in other words, the warp ends are alternately raised or lowered. If you look at your shed and don't see the up-down-up down sequence, check the position of your heddles.

Figure 1. Warp Color Order

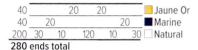

40		20	20		☐ Jaune Or
40	20			20	■ Marine
200	30	10	120	10	30	☐ Natural

280 ends total

Figure 3. Weft Color Order

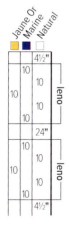

Numbers indicate picks of that color unless followed by the inch symbol ("). In that case, weave that color for as many inches as indicated.

Figure 2. Threading with Two Rigid Heddles

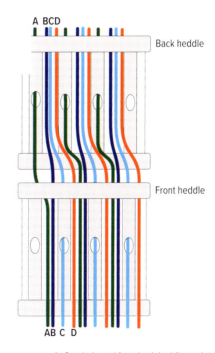

A One hole end from back heddle to slot to its right in front heddle.
B One hole end from back heddle to slot in front heddle.
C One slot end from back heddle to hole to right in front heddle.
D One slot end in back heddle to slot to right in front heddle.

Weaving Pick-up Leno

There are two ways to create leno lace, one with an open shed, then second with a closed shed. In this project, we will be using an open-shed technique that allows the weaver to create a pick-up row, followed by a non pick-up row, what I refer to as the bonus row. Weave each leno section as follows.

1. With your heddles in the Up position, start at the right selvedge and pass your pick-up stick through the open shed until you reach the first blue stripe.

2. With your pick-up stick in your right hand, use your left hand fingertips to push the first two blue threads in the upper position to the left. (See photo **1**.)

3. Pick up the first two blue threads from the bottom layer, place them on the pick-up stick, and allow the first two threads from the top layer to fall below the stick. (See photo **2**.)

4. Use your right index finger to hold the pair of twist threads off to the right as your pick-up the new pair. Repeat until all blue threads have been twisted, creating 5 lace units. (See photo **3**.)

5. Continue passing your pick-up stick to the left through the open shed through the narrow natural stripe, then repeat the 2:2 leno pick-up in the yellow stripe. (See photo **4**.)

6. Pass the pick-up stick through the open shed for the natural-colored center section, then repeat the leno patterning in the yellow and blue stripes as before, passing the pick-up through the open shed in the narrow natural-colored stripe. End by passing the pick-up stick the rest of the way through the open shed. Leave the stick in place. (See photo **5**.)

7. After all threads have been twisted, close the shed, turn the pick-up stick up on end, and pass the shuttle stick with the leno stripe color through the shed created by the pick-up stick. (See photo **6**.)

8. Lay your pick-up stick flat and use it to push this pick against the fell line. You will feel resistance where the warp threads are twisted. Press firmly, but try to avoid too much draw-in at the selvedges. (See photo **7**.)

9. For the next pick, simple change to the opposite plain-weave shed from the previous row and pass your shuttle. The twisted threads will automatically revert to their starting positions, giving the illusion that they are twisting again. (See photo **8**.)

10. Repeat this 2-row pattern five times (5x) to create square lace units in the colored stripes.

1. Pick up and cross first two blue threads.

2. Place crossed threads on pick-up stick.

3. Pick up and twist all threads in the blue stripe.

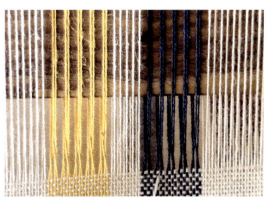

4. Pick up and twist threads in the yellow stripe.

5. Continue across, picking and twisting all colored threads.

6. Turn pick-up stick on its side.

7. Put in weft pick to hold twist.

8. Make a plain-weave pick to finish the twist.

CHAPTER FOUR

NORDIC CRAFTSMANSHIP

Swedish art weaver Gunvor Johansson's samples. Skånes Hemslöjörbund, Landskrona, Sweden. Photo by Veronna Capone.

Left: Detail of acanthus carving on spinning wheel from Gudbrandsdalen, ca. 1870s, author's collection.

That which is loved is always beautiful.

—*Norwegian saying*

Modern Nordic design is recognized around the world for its simplicity, elegance, and the quality of craftsmanship. But these qualities are not new. With the combination of scarce resources and long, dark winters, Scandinavians have always created beauty from what they had—materials that are available to anyone. Humble materials, wood and wool, have been transformed into furniture and household items that also brighten the home. Precious materials, such as silver, have been worked into jewelry and tableware with classic designs that are treasured and handed down through generations.

Since Nordic branding efforts began in the 1950s, the world has been very aware of Scandinavian design and craftsmanship, from art and architecture to cheery, minimalist furnishings from IKEA. But today's designs build on centuries of craftsmanship by rural people, local artisans, and guilds. Here are just a few of the traditions that influence today's designs.

ARTISTRY IN WOOD: ACANTHUS CARVING

The acanthus plant (genus *Acanthae*) is a symbol of immortality and resurrection, and it was first used as a decorative motif by the artisans of ancient Greece. The acanthus leaf motif, most likely modeled on *Acanthus spinosus*, appears on capitals (decorations at the tops of columns) in ancient Greek and Roman buildings throughout the Mediterranean world. In the Christian era, the thorny leaves came to symbolize the pain and suffering of sin, and the style found its way into Byzantine and Gothic architecture, then "flowered" anew during the Renaissance, and again in the designs of the British Arts and Crafts movement in the late nineteenth century.

Bowl in the "Meet the Vikings" exhibition in the Nationalmuseet, Copenhagen, Denmark. Photo by John Capone.

The acanthus motif was adopted by rural Nordic woodworkers in the eighteenth and nineteenth centuries.[23] (Acanthus also figures prominently in rosemaling designs, although in a very stylized form.) Acanthus carving was first used to adorn cornices and paneling in churches, often painted with gilt and bright colors. In homes, the designs were quickly adapted to furniture, wooden drinking vessels, and other household items. According to folk art scholar Janice Stewart, the large designs in bas-relief carving showed up well in rural homes, which, in the eighteenth century, were often still small and relatively dark inside. The antique spinning wheel from Gudbrandsdalen, shown on page 100, is a beautiful example of this style.

During the National Romantic period in the late nineteenth century, acanthus designs, both in carving and rosemaling, enjoyed a renewed popularity in Scandinavia, and once again during the twentieth century through the interest of Scandinavian immigrants to America reclaiming their heritage.

Acanthus spinosus, Cambridge University Botanic Garden. Photo by Magnus Manske, licensed under CC BY-SA 3.0.

Acanthus carved oblong ale bowl with short spout on one end and slightly fan-shaped handle at one end. Norway, ca. 1870–1900. Collection of Vesterheim Norwegian-American Museum, Decorah, Iowa.

Replica of the Baldishol tapestry fragment. Photo by Frode Inge Helland. licensed under CC BY-SA 3.0.

ARTISTRY IN CLOTH

Textiles, too, have long reflected Scandinavian craftsmanship, from Viking times to the present. Textile fragments from the Oseberg ship include pictorial "tapestries" (not what we today would call tapestry, but a form of inlay or brocading), tablet-woven patterned bands and braids, and patterned fabrics of wool and linen.

One of the most famous textiles in Scandinavia is the Baldishol tapestry, a fragment found being used as a rag in a seventeenth-century church in Hedmark, Norway. Beautifully woven and dating to the eleventh or twelfth century, it is part of what was once a larger work. It portrays a bearded man standing by a flowering tree and a horseman, thought to represent April and May, respectively. The Viking Age Överhogdal tapestries, dating to between 1040 and 1170 CE, were also discovered in a rag heap in Sweden in 1910, during the renovation of a local church.

These ancient tapestries were specially woven for important people of their times, but most textile production was the work of the common folk. Rural households devoted a great deal of their energy to producing, washing, processing, spinning, and often dyeing wool and flax for clothing and household textiles.

A wealthy farm might have a building devoted to weaving, and a poorer farm would give up precious space in the small home for it. Until the eighteenth century, a rural weaver would use a warp-weighted loom, made of logs, that could be assembled and set up against a wall, then stowed away until the next season. According to Stewart, the loom would be set up after Christmas, and weaving would be a primary task until spring, when summer tasks took over.[24]

When floor looms came into common use, they occupied a place of pride in the farmhouse or weaving shed. While shirts and undergarments were made of simple cloth, coverlets and wall hangings were an opportunity to show the weaver's skill and add color to the home. Intricately patterned *krokbragd*, the patterning called Vestfoldsmett in Norway and "art weaving" in Sweden, the bright geometric dukagang patterns of Sweden, and the overshot patterning known as skillbragd or opphämta (see page 65) all graced beds and walls, keeping the family warm and brightening dark interiors.

FROM FOLK ART TO ART

Among the most prized household textiles were tapestries, which might be used as wall hangings or bedcovers. These were more likely to be found in prosperous households, bought from a weaver who specialized in the clasped-weft technique[25] called *billedvev*, or "picture weave." The stylized images in the tapestry coverlets often had biblical themes, and one of the most popular was the story of the wise and foolish virgins. As the story goes, when ten virgins went to greet the celestial Bridegroom, five brought enough oil for their lamps and five brought too little and had to go home instead. (A lesson in Nordic practicality: one can see why this theme was so popular.)

In the nineteenth-century National Romantic period, this folk craft turned to art. In the *Norwegian Textile Newsletter*,[26] Vesterheim chief curator Laurann Gilbertson and Kathleen Stokker tell the amazing story of the Baldishol tapestry. The piece was acquired by the Oslo Museum of Applied Art, and many women, inspired by Norway's oldest tapestry, took up tapestry weaving. One of these was Ragna Breivik, born in 1891, a farm girl and daughter of a renowned weaver, who trained at a women's industrial arts school in Oslo, worked in a tapestry atelier, and studied at the Arts and Handicrafts school in Bergen.[27] In the 1890s Norwegian landscape painter Gerhard Munthe created a series of Arts and Crafts style

Detail of a runner woven with traditional coverlet techniques by the author.

Three Brothers, tapestry woven from a painting by Gerhard Munthe Weaver unknown, 1908. Oslo, Norway. Collection of Vesterheim Norwegian-American Museum, Decorah, Iowa.

Carpet woven by Märta Måås-Fjetterström, date unknown. Collection of Doris Leslie Blau, under CC BY-SA 3.0.

paintings to illustrate the *Heimskringla*, the heroic folktales of the Icelandic politician and poet Snori Sturluson. These paintings inspired artisan designs in silver, woodcarving, and porcelain, and tapestries based on the paintings became something of an industry for professional weavers. Ragna Breivik devoted her career to weaving tapestries of Munthe's paintings, ten of which, called the Åsmund Frægdagjeva cycle, now hang in the Horda Museum in her native district of Fana. While Munthe somewhat resented the popularity that his work gained when interpreted in wool, he is most remembered for the work of Breivik and other weavers who rendered his art in tapestry.

Another weaver, Märta Måås-Fjetterström, turned the craft of rug weaving into art. Born in Kimstad, Sweden, in 1873, she attended the Högre School of Arts, Crafts, and Design in Stockholm. She was interested in traditional folk textiles, and early in her career, like Ragna Breivik, she wove decorative tapestry on traditional themes. But she found her lifelong artistic focus in designing and weaving rugs, including *rya* (pile) rugs, and *rölaken* (square weave) rugs, all techniques from the Scandinavian folk tradition. Her designs combined a twentieth-century modern aesthetic with images from nature, landscapes, and folk textiles, as well as spare geometric designs that would be at home in a Bauhaus building. Her rugs are prized around the world: one is even used in the Nobel Prize ceremony. She is one of Sweden's most famous and influential textile artists, and the rug-weaving studio she founded in Båstad, Sweden, is still weaving and selling her designs today to textile lovers all over the world.

THE BEAUTY OF BANDS

Woven bands are an important part of Nordic history and culture. They appear in archeological finds going back to the Viking Age, and some scholars date finds of band-weaving equipment back to the late Stone Age. Reconstructed garments of Viking chieftains and nobles show how their clothes were embellished with brocaded bands of silk and gold and silver threads, precious imports from trade with the Middle East. And tablet-weaving expert Sonja Berlin relates how tablet weaving was used for ecclesiastical textiles in the Middle Ages, in part because weavers could produce lettering long before the printing press was invented.[28]

Up through the Industrial Age, bands were a part of everyday Scandinavian life. They were used to swaddle babies and to embellish garments and hats, and they served as ties for aprons, bonnets, and bags.[29] For the Indigenous Sámi

peoples of the Nordic North, band weaving still holds an important place in their handicraft tradition or *duodji*. In her book *Weaving Patterned Bands*, Susan Foulkes relates how the Sámi weave bands to trim clothing and small bags, and how they tie bands around their fur boots to keep the snow out. The band patterns and colors indicate a person's village, family, marital status, and gender.[30]

Band weaving was also an important cottage industry. Foulkes relates a saying from Leksand, Sweden, that "one should weave 2 to 3 meters while boiling the potatoes."[31] I think either those band weavers were lightning fast or those were tough potatoes! (Susan's theory is that they were exaggerating, and she is a band weaver par excellence, so I trust her judgment.)

There are three traditional band-weaving techniques in Scandinavia: tablet or card weaving, *grind* weaving, and finger weaving. Sonja Berlin uses the Swedish word *brickvävning* for the tablet-weaving technique, but each Scandinavian country and region has its own names. In the past, tablet weaving used square, thin pieces of wood, bone, horn, or even stone (lignite) with holes usually punched in each of the corners; today's tablet weavers often use cards made of heavy paper stock. Warp yarns of different colors are threaded through the holes in the tablets. The threads are tensioned on a loom or between a post and the weaver's belt, and the cards are rotated to bring different colors to the surface of the band and create patterns.

In *grind* weaving, a small rigid heddle is used to raise and lower the warp threads for weaving. Often band weavers used a *spaltegrind*, or double-slotted heddle, in which some of the heddle dents have holes like a normal rigid heddle, and some have short slots to hold the pattern threads (these are variously called *spaltegrind*, *bandgrind*, or, by Sámi weavers, a Sunna heddle). Grind weavers would often use a small loom resembling a tiny cradle, typically embellished with rosemaling or carving. Cradle looms are portable, and weaving materials can be conveniently tucked inside when the loom is not in use.

The third method for making bands is a type of flat braiding. Although the

Handwoven bands in the Vesterheim collection. The chevron band in the center is an example of *fletting* (flat braiding or fingerweaving). Photo by Anita Osterhaug. Collection of Vesterheim Norwegian-American Museum, Decorah, Iowa.

technique is sometimes called finger weaving, there is no separate warp and weft. Instead, the threads pass through each other, alternately acting as warp or weft. In fact, the traditional Norwegian word for this technique, *fletting*, is used today to refer to very elaborate hair braiding popular with young women. (There are even online tutorials. Google it. You'll be amazed!) These fletted bands were most often used as garters for holding up stockings, but if you want to try the technique, there are instructions for a finger-woven braid in the "Why Knot? Market Bag" project (see page 164).

STICKS AND STRANDS: SCANDINAVIAN KNITTING

According to Susanne Pagoldh, knitting came to the Nordic countries in the sixteenth and seventeenth centuries, with the introduction of imported knit silk stockings and sweaters, available to a wealthy few.[32] As with other techniques and styles of ornamentation, the knitted styles and patterns were quickly copied by everyday Scandinavians and incorporated into folk costume. Although knitting was slower than weaving, it could be done year-round, and knitted garments were practical for working people.

Pagoldh says that knitting pattern books, adapted from embroidery patterns, were available in Scandinavia in the sixteenth century. The early knitted garments tended to be a single color, and designs were created with delicate cables, patterns of purl stitches on a stockinette stitch background, or, later, with lace. Dyeing with natural dyes was time consuming and unreliable, and the colors tended to

Two-color knitted mittens, Selbu Bygdemusem, Selby, Norway. Selbu proclaims itself as the home of two-color knitting. (Although other parts of Scandinavia might disagree.) Photo by John Capone.

fade, so color patterning was used sparingly. Garments in the natural colors of sheep's wool would be accented with bits of precious, usually professionally dyed red yarn. (In Scandinavian culture, "the red thread" is the spark, the thing that ties everything else together.) Smaller items, such as gloves or stockings, might be knitted with multiple colors in subtle patterns, especially at the cuffs, and two-end knitting (*tvåändsstickning*) was used in all the mainland Nordic countries, to produce tight, hard-wearing fabric.

The bright, multicolor patterning we associate with Nordic sweaters didn't become common until the nineteenth century, when aniline dyes became available and affordable. From this period came the familiar stripes; "lice"-patterned sweaters (patterned with dots), or *lusekofta*; eight-pointed stars, probably adopted from Middle Eastern textiles; and other geometric patterns we associate with Scandinavian knitting today.

Scandinavians still prize craftsmanship in their sweaters. I'll never forget being stopped by a group of local ladies at an open-air history museum in Norway. They were interested in my sweater, one that my grandmother had brought back from a trip to Norway. I had to take it off and turn it inside out so that they could inspect the knitting and finishing on both sides. When they saw the knitted interfacings, they finally approved. And the sweater is made to last for generations, so maybe my grandchildren will have a similar experience when they visit the "old country" someday.

The author's father at Reed College in a Norwegian sweater probably knitted by his older sister Kathryn, 1950s. (Lookin' good, Dad.)

SHINE LIKE THE SUN: SCANDINAVIAN SILVERWORK

Metalworking in Scandinavia dates back at least to the Bronze Age, as evidenced by the Trundholm sun chariot (shown in chapter 1). Viking Age relics show metalworking skills and an appreciation for fine work, influenced by the metal ornaments brought back to Scandinavia through raid or trade. The Vikings prized silver, in particular, and the Viking Age is sometimes called the Silver Age.

Through the Middle Ages and onward, metalworking continued to be the province of artisans. But scholar Janice Stewart says it was not until the Renaissance that fine metalworking skills were common in rural Scandinavia. By the seventeenth century, mines in mountainous Norway were producing iron ore, copper, and silver for export to the rest of Europe. Skilled metalworkers were brought from Germany to Scandinavian cities to turn these metals into marketable goods.[33]

Left: Silver bridal crown, ca. 1740. Bergen, Hordaland, Norway. Collection of Vesterheim Norwegian-American Museum, Decorah, Iowa.

Right: Norwegian folk dress worn with two intricate sølje. Setesdal, Norway, ca. 1865. Collection of Vesterheim Norwegian-American Museum, Decorah, Iowa.

In farm and city houses alike, fancy iron hinges and gleaming copper kettles became a point of pride.

But silverwork was the most prized, the most magical product of the metalworker's art. Silver clasps, brooches, buckles, and pins became an essential part of folk costume. Certain pieces, such as the silver crown worn by a bride or the groom's cross-shaped pendant, were specifically used for church ceremonies, but all silver jewelry was considered to have a certain holiness and power. Stewart relates a legend in which a kidnapped girl is adorned with silver by the *huldrefolk* (the hidden folk, or elves) who live under the mountain for a wedding to one of their own. Her human sweetheart rescues her and marries her in a church, and the huldrefolk place a curse on the enterprising couple for making off with their precious silver.[34] Rikard Berge, writing in the early 1920s, related that a silver buckle might be fastened to a baby's swaddling band "so the trolls won't exchange babies," and a collection of nine pieces of heirloom or church silver would protect against "troll love."[35] (I wonder whether this is a euphemism for falling in love with an unsuitable person. In any case, there were obviously more trolls at large then than now.)

The Sølje

The *sølje* brooch is considered the national jewelry of Norway. These graceful brooches have been an integral part of Norwegian folk tradition for centuries. Made of sterling silver, these round or heart-shaped brooches feature fine filigree work, and many have dangling disks to represent the sun. A small sølje is often the silver pinned to a baby's christening blanket or pillow to ward off trolls and other harm. A young woman may receive a more elaborate sølje when she comes of age, or have one handed down to her upon her marriage. Women, including the Sámi, will wear one or more sølje with their national costumes, and men sometimes also wear sølje as shoe buckles.

SØLJE CURTAINS TO CELEBRATE THE SUN

by BIRGIT ALBIKER-OSTERHAUG

CRAFT: *Knitting*

DIFFICULTY LEVEL: *Intermediate*

When Anita suggested a valance for this project, I envisioned an airy and playful piece with repeating motifs centered on a simple lace background. The famous *sølje* brooches as well as the popular jacket fasteners or belt buckles are obvious choices for inspiration. I was intrigued by the intricate details worked into the examples displayed in the Vesterheim collection, since they challenged me to apply many different knitting skills.

Structure: Lace knitting

Materials

Yarn Aunt Lydia's Crochet Thread Fashion 3 (100% mercerized cotton; 150 yd [137 m]): White, 1 ball for each 60-row rep (see Notes).

Needles Sizes 1½ (2.5 mm) and 2½ (3 mm): 24" circular (cir). Adjust needle size if necessary to obtain the correct gauge.

Notions Markers (m); 12 size 6/0 (size E) seed beads for each 60-row rep (see Notes); size 9 (1.25 mm) steel crochet hook (must fit through hole in beads); blocking wires and pins; tapestry needle.

Gauge 24 sts and 44 rows = 4" in garter st on smaller needle; 26 sts and 44 rows = 4" in patt on smaller needle.

Dimensions

Finished Size: 19" high; each 60-row rep measures 5½" wide.

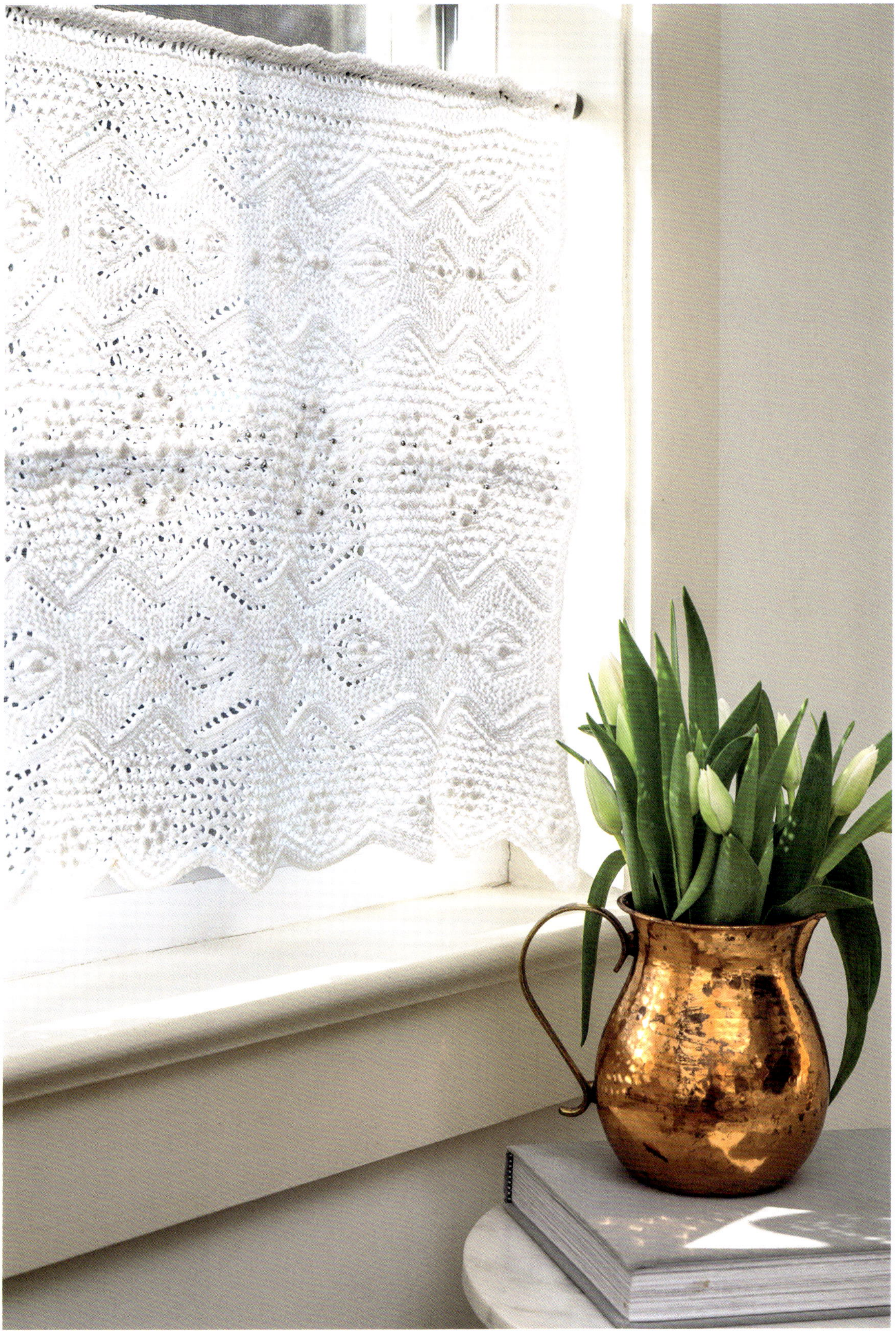

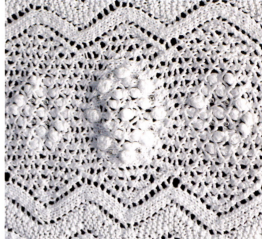

Left: Inspiration for the large center motif. Sølje by Jacob Ulrich Holfeldt Tostrup. Oslo, Norway, ca. 1890. Collection of Vesterheim Norwegian-American Museum, Decorah, Iowa.

I decided to focus on a center motif patterned after a particular brooch in the collection, framed by a belt buckle, also in the collection, of the popular diamond shape used in many of the silver jacket closures. The motifs are accented in waving knitted bands simulating the border details in some of the Norwegian carvings. The brooch details inspired me to use a variety of stitches and beads, and different variations of nupps and bobbles.

1900–1930. Collection of Vesterheim Norwegian-American Museum, Decorah, Iowa

The valance is worked back and forth from left to right with a repeating pattern of sixty rows to allow for variations in your window width. I used a ladder stitch for a top border so you can hang the valance with a rod or hooks. However, alternative edge stitches may be used or the ladder stitch can be eliminated if desired. The height of the piece can be shortened by eliminating one of the motifs above or below the center or by inserting additional center or side motifs. Each element is charted separately, which makes it easier to lengthen or shorten the project. Note: When varying the height of the piece, adjust the last stitch(es) of the remaining charts to match the pattern of the lace background.

I chose a mercerized cotton crochet thread in size 3 to provide stability and sheen. Each pattern repeat of sixty rows uses just under one ball of thread. The popular brand Aunt Lydia 3 is available in many different colors.

Notes
- This rectangular valance is worked back and forth from end to end.
- The hole in the beads must be large enough to accommodate two strands of crochet cotton. Choose beads that are machine-washable if you will be machine-washing the valance.
- When working nupps, work the stitches loosely. This will give a better shape to the nupp and will make it easier to purl the stitches together on the wrong-side row.
- Each 60-row repeat uses just under one ball of crochet cotton.
- A circular needle is used to accommodate the large number of stitches.

Stitch Guide
Knitted cast-on: Make a slipknot and place it onto left needle (counts as a st). K1 into slipknot and transfer new st to left needle kwise. *K1 into first st on left needle and transfer new st to left needle kwise; rep from * until desired number of sts are CO.

Make Bobble: ([K1, p1] 2 times, k1) into same st; [transfer 5 sts to left needle, k5] 2 times, pass 2nd, 3rd, 4th, and 5th sts over first st.

Place Bead: Slide bead onto crochet hook. Insert crochet hook pwise into st and sl st onto crochet hook. Slide bead down hook onto st, then return st to left needle and knit it.

Splicing: Aunt Lydia Crochet Thread Fashion 3 is a 3-ply yarn. To splice, separate yarn into 3 strands for 3" on both old and new yarn. Twist together 1 strand of old yarn with 2 strands of new yarn for 3". Keep remaining strands on WS of piece. Work across transition from old yarn to spliced yarn to new yarn. Before blocking, either break remaining strands or weave them in separately on WS of piece.

Instructions
With larger needle and using the knitted method, CO 123 sts. Change to smaller needle.

Set-up row (WS): K22, place marker (pm), k17, pm, k39, pm, k17, pm, k28.

Next row (RS): Work Lower Edging chart over 28 sts, sl m, work Side Motif chart over 17 sts, sl m, work Center Motif chart over 39 sts, sl m, work Side Motif chart over 17 sts, sl m, work Upper Edge chart over 22 sts.

Cont in patt until rows 1–60 of charts have been worked 4 times, or to desired width, ending with row 60 of charts.

Cont in patt, work rows 1 and 2 of charts again.

Knit 1 RS row. Change to larger needle. Knit 1 WS row. Loosely BO all sts kwise.

Finishing
Weave in ends. Block using blocking wires for sides and top, and pins for scalloped lower edge.

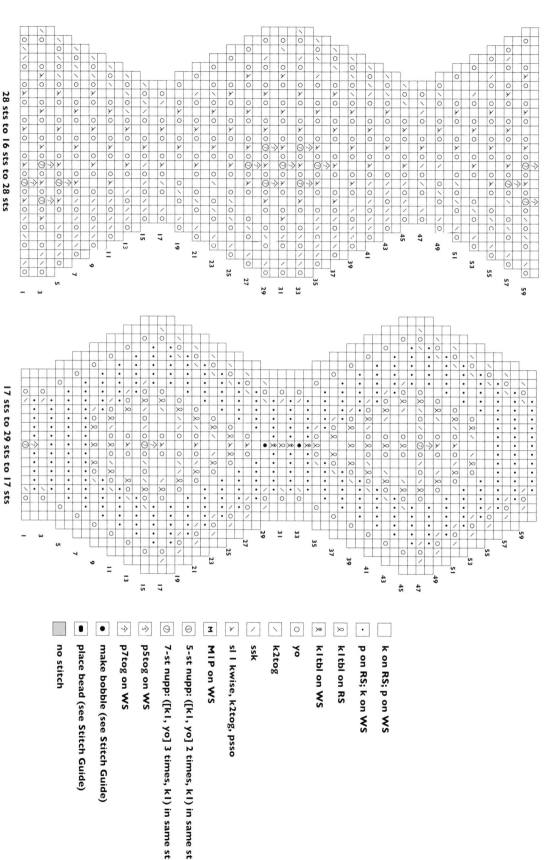

Figure 1. Lower Edging Chart

28 sts to 16 sts to 28 sts

Figure 2. Side Motif Chart

17 sts to 29 sts to 17 sts

	k on RS; p on WS
·	p on RS; k on WS
⋋	k1 tbl on RS
⋈	k1 tbl on WS
○	yo
⋌	k2tog
⋋	ssk
⋋	sl 1 kwise, k2tog, psso
M	M1P on WS
⊘	5-st nupp: ([k1, yo] 2 times, k1) in same st
⊘	7-st nupp: ([k1, yo] 3 times, k1) in same st
⟿	p5tog on WS
⤳	p7tog on WS
●	make bobble (see Stitch Guide)
●	place bead (see Stitch Guide)
▨	no stitch

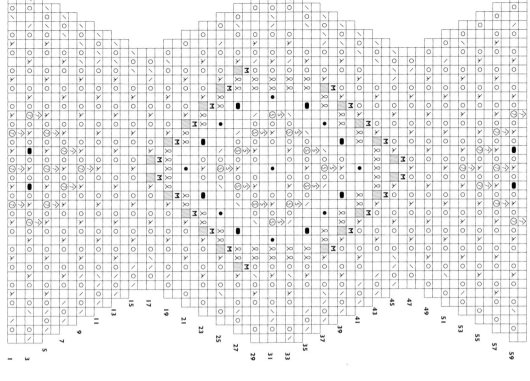

Figure 3. Center Motif Chart

39 sts to 27 sts to 39 sts

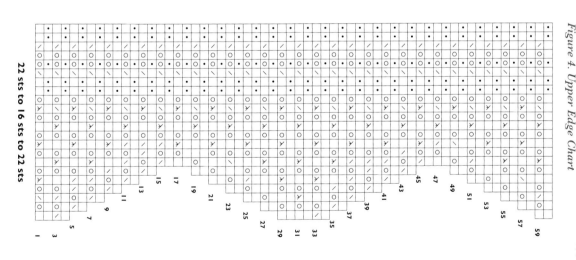

Figure 4. Upper Edge Chart

22 sts to 16 sts to 22 sts

HANDSOME DANSKBROGD PILLOWS

by JAN MOSTROM

CRAFT: *Weaving*

DIFFICULTY LEVEL: *Advanced beginner*

Like other aspects of Nordic folk art, Scandinavian weaving is rich with regional and local variations, whose origins are sometimes buried in the mists of time. For instance, the lovely and versatile weave called *danskbrogd*, or "Danish weave," may have come from Denmark by some long-forgotten route, but since at least the eighteenth century, it has been woven in a small area in the south of Vest Agder, Norway. Danskbrogd is a bound weave or weft-faced weave, meaning that the warp threads are completely covered by the weft and do not show in the pattern.

The geometric designs in danskbrogd, small contrasting blocks, are created by picking specific warp threads in a shed up or down, so that they can be covered by different-colored weft yarns. The danskbrogd pattern shows up against a weft-faced plain weave or krokbragd pattern, often combined in a single piece. While danskbrogd patterning is traditionally arranged in variations of diamonds, Xs, and zigzags, contemporary weavers have used this technique to weave designs of trees, flowers, bees and honeycombs, and even pictorial elements within a tapestry. The possibilities are endless!

Structure: Weft-face plain weave with danskbrogd pick-up designs

Equipment
Rigid-heddle loom, 20" weaving width; 8-dent heddles; 4 stick shuttles, 20"–24" long; sharp-edged pick-up stick, at least 22" long.

Materials
Yarns

Warp: 12/6 cotton seine twine, also called *fiskgarn* (1,400 yd/lb; Bockens), Natural, 400 yd.

Weft: Rauma Prydvevgarn 6/2 weight (100% Norwegian Spælsau wool; 300 meters/100 gm skein; Blue Heron Knittery), #605 Medium gray, 2 skeins; #636 Black, 150 m (165 yd); #635 Red, 60 m (66 yd); #601 White 90 m (99 yd).

Optional: #603, Light gray 19 m (20 yd) for random stripes in the medium gray sections.

Other supplies: Rags, thick waste yarn, or flat sticks to spread the warp and space the warp between the pillow tops; wool or other fabric for pillow backing, 20" square for each pillow; sewing machine and thread to match pillow and backing; two 18"–20" pillow forms, depending how firm you want the stuffing.

Warp Length

157 ends 2½ yd (90") long (allows 6" for take-up, 30" for loom waste).

Setts

Warp: 8 epi.

Weft: About 44 ppi in solid areas; about 66 ppi in pattern sections.

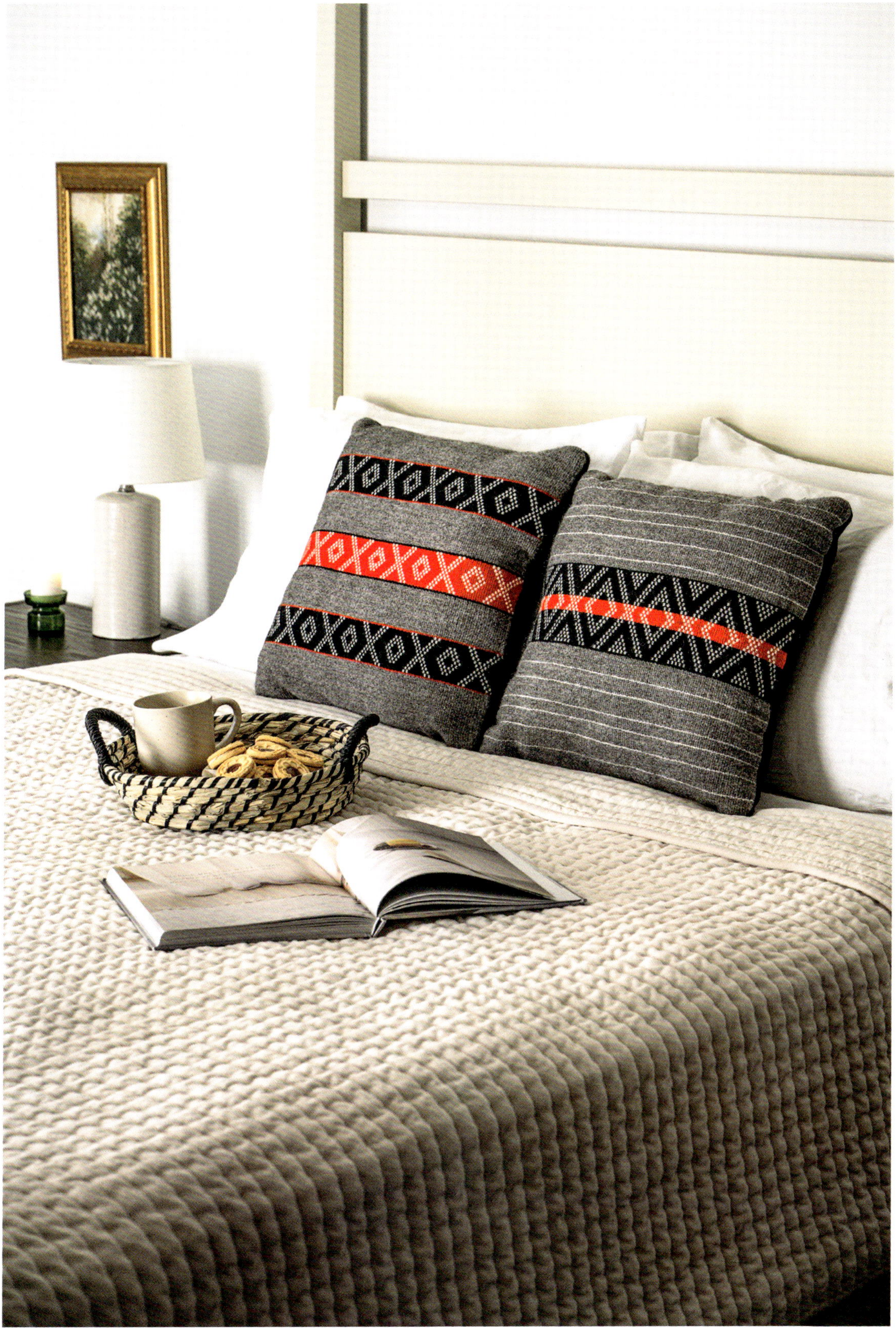

Dimensions

Width in the heddle: 19⅝".

Woven length: (measured under tension on the loom) 54".

Finished size: (after wet-finishing and hemming) Two pillow covers, 18" by 18".

You can read more about danskbrogd in my article "Weaving Danskbrogd," in the *Norwegian Textile Newsletter* 28, no. 1, Feb. 2022.

Instructions

1. Set up your loom for direct warping a length of 90" or wind a warp of 157 ends 2½ yd long. Warp the loom using your preferred method, centering for a weaving width of 19⁶⁄₈".

2. Wind stick shuttles with the weft colors.

3. Spread the warp with rags, thick yarn, or sticks, leaving at least 10" before the pillows. then begin weaving the first pillow. (See the weft color sequence in figure 1). Weave 8" of plain weave in medium gray. If you choose, you can add in some random 2-shot stripes of light gray to add interest. After closing the shed, open the next shed and use the pick-up stick to pack in the previous weft pick before putting in the next one. If needed, you can also use the tines of a table fork to beat the weft so that it is covering all the warps snugly. (You can weave a little extra gray at the beginning and end of each pillow to ensure you can center your stripe design when you sew the pillows. The woven length shrinks a little when the fabric is taken off the loom and is no longer under tension.)

4. Weave 4 shots of black, then begin the danskbrogd pick-up pattern as shown in figure 2. See the inset for the weaving sequence. When you get to the 10th row, change your background color to red for 5 pattern rows. Pay attention to how the white pattern spots sit on the black and red backgrounds so that they match at both transitions. After weaving all rows of pattern, end with 4 shots of black, then repeat the large gray area to match the beginning of your pillow, centering your design stripe.

Figure 1. Weft Color Orders

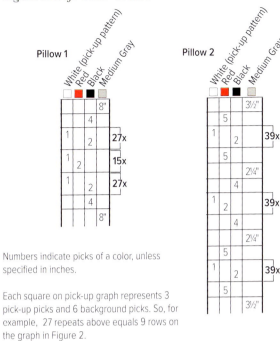

Numbers indicate picks of a color, unless specified in inches.

Each square on pick-up graph represents 3 pick-up picks and 6 background picks. So, for example, 27 repeats above equals 9 rows on the graph in Figure 2.

Figure 2. Pick-up Patterns

Each row represents 3 pick-up picks and 6 background picks. Weave both patterns bottom to top.

Pillow 1 pick-up pattern

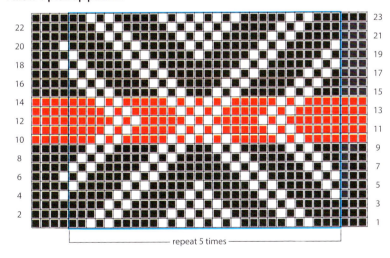

repeat 5 times

Pillow 2 pick-up pattern

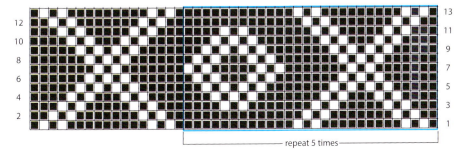

repeat 5 times

5. After weaving a header, weave enough length between the pillows with flat sticks or rags to allow for tying knots at the end of each pillow. A gap of 8"–10" should be about right.

6. Weave the second pillow, using the same techniques as for the first. (See figure 1 for the weft color order.) First, weave $3^1/_2$" of medium gray in plain weave, beating as before. Weave 5 picks of red, then the first pattern band, following the graph in figure 2, with white pattern spots on a black background, and finish with 4 picks of red. Next, weave $2^1/_4$" of medium gray. Weave the second pattern band with white design spots on a red background bordered by 4 picks of black at the beginning and end. Weave another $2^1/_4$" of medium gray, then weave the third pattern band identical to the first. Finish by weaving $3^1/_2$" of medium gray, then weave rags, yarn, or sticks for a header.

7. Cut the fabric from the loom, leaving the headers in place to protect the ends.

Assembling the Pillows

1. After taking the weaving off the loom, tie overhand knots in the warp ends in groups of 3 or 4. Trim the warp threads to about an inch from the knots.

2. Choose a firm fabric for your backing. Felted wool, upholstery fabric, or heavy linen are good choices. Cut the backing to match the size of the pillow top. Double-check and mark with pins where to sew your seams in order to square your pillow and center your stripe designs.

3. With right sides together, sew fronts and backs together, leaving one side partially open to insert your pillow form. It is helpful to put a piece of masking tape near the sewing line to cover the floats on the back of the pick-up stripes so that they do not catch on the presser foot when you are sewing the seams. To avoid having dog-eared corners, round your corners about $^1/_2$" in from the corner instead of making a sharp right angle.

4. Trim a corner off the backing at each corner and turn your pillow right side out.

5. Steam the seams so that they are flat and neat. Press the seam allowances at the opening to make it easier to handsew the seam closed.

6. Insert your pillow form. Handstitch the opening with a hidden stitch such as mattress stitch.

7. Put your pillows on a chair or sofa. Sit back and admire.

Weaving the Danskbrogd Pattern

To weave the danskbrogd patterns, you will be using the pick-up stick in the bottom layer of the shed. Each square of the chart represents a warp thread. Each row consists of three steps repeated three times (see photos). The steps are:

1. Open a shed. Counting carefully and working from beneath the bottom layer, use the pick-up stick to push down each warp end that has an X in the chart. Count carefully and double-check. (See photo **1**.) Turn your pick-up stick on its side to create a new shed. Throw a shot of white in the shed you have created. (See photo **2**.) Remove the stick and beat in the white. (See photo **3**.)

2. Open the same shed as before. Now you will be using the pick-up stick to push down all of the other warp threads in that layer, or you might find it easier to think of picking up the warps that have already been covered with the white weft. Turn your stick on edge and insert a background weft shot in the newly created shed. Remove the stick and beat in the weft shot. Every warp in the bottom layer of the shed should now be covered.

3. Change to the opposite shed, weave a pick with the background weft, and beat. Now you have covered every warp thread once.

Repeat these three steps 3 times for each pattern row.

1. Pick down warp ends to be covered by white.

2. Turn pick-up stick on its side and insert white weft pick.

3. Beat down white weft.

Notes

*   If the counting does not work out, you may be in the wrong shed. Try going to the opposite shed so that the threads that need to be covered are in the bottom layer of the shed.
*   When you are ready to begin a new pattern row and are in the shed that will need pick-up, check to see that there is already a background weft above the white pattern spot you have just completed. If there is, you can begin the pick-up work. If there is no background above the white, weave a background weft, change the shed, and weave another background shot. Now you are back to the shed that needs to be picked, and since the white design spot now has one background shot above it you may pick the new design row. Watching for that background weft above the patten spot spaces all of the design spots correctly. Otherwise, some of the design spots will touch at the corners and some will not which would distort the design.
*   Always double-check your counting. This takes much less time than taking out a picking mistake. Remember you will only use the pick-up stick in the bottom layer of the shed.

A NORDIC SWEATER FOR YOUR LAPTOP

by DEB CARPENTER-BECK

CRAFT: *Knitting*
DIFFICULTY LEVEL: *Intermediate*

I like computer bags that are both functional and stylish. For years, I've enjoyed doing Scandinavian stranded knitting, and in recent years I've also gotten into weaving, so this project combines two of my favorite things!

The inspiration for this three-color bag was a navy-blue, red, and white border motif from a handwoven Swedish opphämta curtain, housed in the textile collection of the American Swedish Institute (see page 124). I enlarged and simplified the pattern for knitting and changed the red background color to a more subtle teal. Each side of the bag is worked upward from the base and knit back and forth in rows, rather than in the round, to provide side seams for greater stability. To add further structure and protection for a laptop computer, I lined the bag with navy-blue felt fabric, easily found in your local sewing store or online.

While the sample bag has rectangular wooden handles that require additional steps, it can also be made with other handles that can be more easily attached. I've included instructions for both. Use this bag as a handy and beautiful way to carry your laptop to and from work or your local coffee shop.

Structure: Stranded knitting

Materials

Yarn Rauma 3-tråds Strikkegarn (100% wool; distributed by The Yarn Guys: 118 yd [108 m] / 1.75 oz [50 g]:

> **MC:** #149 Dark Blue, 2 balls plus 1 extra ball for swatching
>
> **CC1:** #100 White, 2 balls
>
> **CC2:** #175 Sea Green, 1 ball

Needles Size 4 (3.5 mm): 24" circular (cir). Adjust needle size if necessary to obtain the correct gauge. If using rectangular wooden handles, as shown in sample, you will need one additional size 4 (3.5 mm) 24" cir needle for working lining flaps.

Notions Markers (m); rectangular wooden handles or leather handles; 2 stitch holders, if using rectangular wooden handles; contrasting waste yarn for open CO (about 22"); about ½ yd navy blue felt fabric for bag lining; navy blue sewing thread for lining; sewing needle; pins.

Gauge 22 sts and 26 rows = 4" in stranded knitting patt.

Dimensions

Finished Size: 11½" tall by 17" wide, excluding handle. Bag fits most standard laptop computers.

Detail of opphämta hanging. Collection of the American Swedish Institute.

Notes

- The bag is worked back and forth in rows from the bottom up, beginning with a provisional cast-on. It is lined with felt fabric and handles are attached.
- There is a wide choice of wooden or leather handles available to add that perfect finishing touch to your computer bag. Most handles form an open-ended "arch" that allows you to easily attach them to the front of each side of this bag without covering its pattern. For the sample bag, however, I chose four-sided rectangular wooden handles. I loved the look of the handles but attaching them to the front of the bag's sides would have covered the middle diamond pattern. Instead, I attached the handles to the lining and devised a way to "knit around" the handles for the lining flap. The main instructions show you how to work with rectangular handles, but there are additional directions if you prefer to use more standard handles.

Stitch Guide

Open cast-on: With MC and waste yarn held tog, make a slipknot about 2" from end and place onto right needle (does not count as a st). Holding yarns in left hand with waste yarn over index finger and MC over thumb, *bring tip of needle down between the two yarns and pick up MC from behind, then bring needle tip up, over, and behind waste yarn; reach under waste yarn, pick up MC from behind, and bring needle up behind waste yarn and then to front—2 MC sts on needle; rep from * until desired number of sts are CO. Drop slipknot from needle at end of first row of knitting.

Instructions, Bag with Rectangular Handles
Side 1:

With waste yarn, MC, and using the Open method (see Stitch Guide), CO 93 sts.

Working back and forth in St st, work Rows 1–72 of color chart.

With MC, work 2 rows in St st, then purl 1 RS row for lining flap turning ridge.

Dec row (WS): P2tog, purl to last 2 sts, ssp—91 sts rem.

Place sts on holder.

Side 2:

With RS facing, remove waste yarn from open CO and place 93 sts onto needle.

With MC and WS facing, knit 1 row to create a turning ridge (this will be bottom of bag).

Working in St st, work Rows 1–72 of color chart. With MC, work 2 rows in St st, then purl 1 RS row for lining flap turning ridge.

Figure 1. Knitting Color Chart

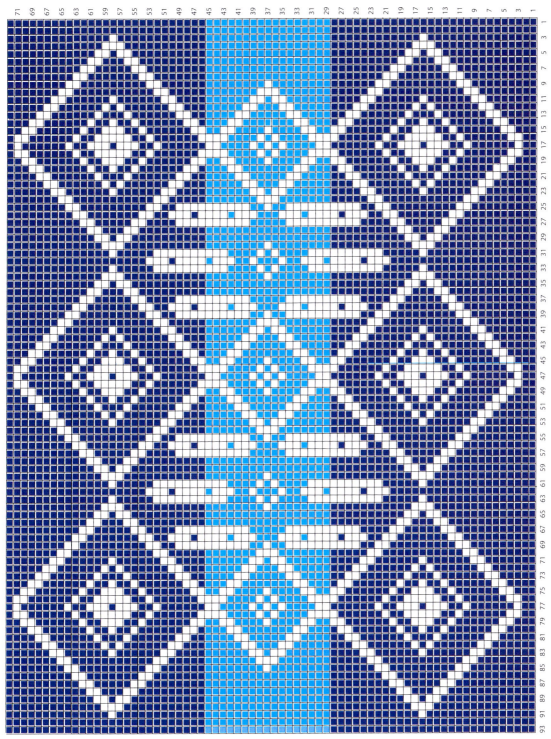

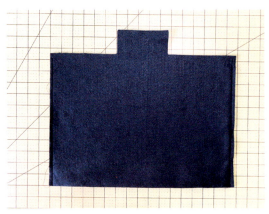

1. Fold bag lining and sew ½" seam up both sides.

2. Fold handle wrap over handle and sew into place.

Dec row (WS): P2tog, purl to last 2 sts, ssp—91 sts rem.

Place sts on holder.

Finishing

Weave in ends. Block to measurements.

Fold along bag's bottom turning ridge so WS of side 1 and side 2 are tog. Sew sides from fold to base of lining flap turning ridge.

Bag Lining

Fold felt fabric in half and cut to measurements shown in photo **1**, including rectangular handle wrap at top. Keep lining folded and sew a ½" seam up each side.

Place one handle (RS facing you) on WS of one side of lining. Fold 2" handle wrap over bottom of handle, pin, then sew into place by hand close to bottom of handle (see photo **2**). Rep for other side of lining.

Place lining into bag with WS tog and sew to bag just below turning ridge, skipping handles.

Lining Flaps

With cir needle and RS facing, transfer sts from holder as foll: Sl 24 sts to needle, pm, sl 37 sts, pm, sl 30 sts—91 sts on needle.

Next row (RS): With 2nd needle and MC, **knit to m, remove m, sl 1 pwise wyf, *sl 1 pwise wyb, psso; rep from * 5 more times (6 BO sts in front of handle), transfer last st on right needle to left needle, turn work; using the cable method and working in front of handle, CO 7 sts as foll: *insert right needle between first and 2nd st on left needle, wrap yarn as if to knit and pull through, then transfer st kwise to left needle; rep from * 6 more times, turn work; sl 1 pwise wyb, pass last CO st over; rep from ** once more, knit to end—1 hole around each side of handle.

Beg with a WS row, work 7 rows in St st.

Loosely BO all sts.

Weave in ends. Fold lining flap over top of lining and sew into place by hand. Rep for other side of bag.

Instructions, Bag with Alternate Handles

Side 1:
Work as for bag with rectangular handles through dec row—91 sts rem.

Lining Flap
Work 8 rows in St st.

Loosely BO all sts.

Side 2:

Work as for bag with rectangular handles through dec row—91 sts rem.

Lining Flap

Work 8 rows in St st.

Loosely BO all sts.

Finishing

Weave in ends. Block to measurements.

Fold along bag's bottom turning ridge so WS of side 1 and side 2 are tog. Sew sides from fold to top of lining flap.

Bag Lining

Fold felt fabric in half and cut to measurements shown in Figure 2, omitting rectangular handle wrap. Keep lining folded and sew a $1/2$" seam up each side. Place lining into bag with WS tog and sew to bag just below turning ridge.

Attach handles to front of each side of bag. Fold lining flap over top of lining and sew into place.

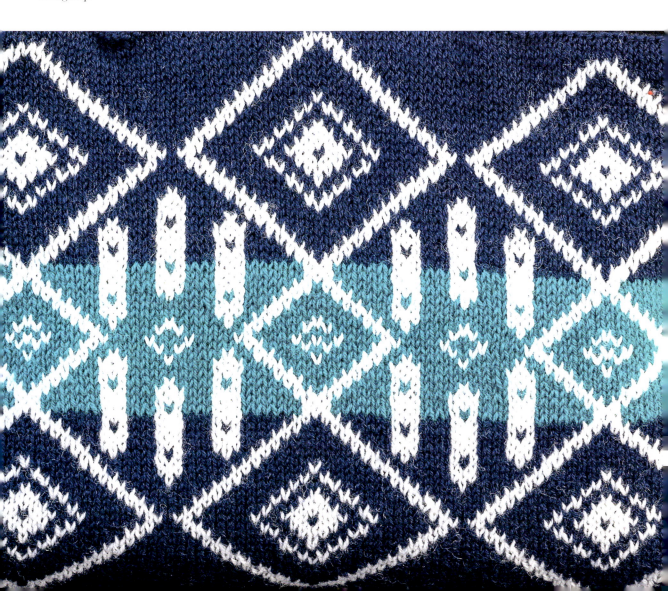

ACANTHUS IN LACE

by BIRGIT ALBIKER-OSTERHAUG

CRAFT: *Knitting*

DIFFICULTY LEVEL: *Intermediate*

The Vesterheim collection includes many items displaying the long history of woodworking in Scandinavia. Whether on ships, churches, furniture, or kitchenware, Nordic carving shows both geometric patterns as well as flowing waves of scrolls, rounded leaves, fans, and other shapes found in nature. I wanted to create a piece that interprets these shapes in the lightness of lace.

This project is created from the center outward in four equal sections, forming a square. Sections are divided by a lace and cable combination and finished with a lace edging, incorporating the triangle often found particularly in older carvings. Lace is also used to create accents between and within motifs. Sections are tied together by a fan extending on both sides of the dividing cable.

Structure: Lace knitting

Materials

Yarn Aunt Lydia's Crochet Thread Classic 10 (100% mercerized cotton; 350 yd [320 m]): Maize, 2 balls.

Needles Sizes 1½ (2.5 mm) and 2½ (3 mm): 24" circular (cir). Adjust needle size if necessary to obtain the correct gauge.

Notions Markers (m); cable needle (cn); size 7 (1.65 mm) steel crochet hook; pins for blocking; tapestry needle.

Gauge 33 sts and 48 rnds = 4" in St st.

Dimensions
Finished Size: 20" square.

Lathe-turned tumbler with acanthus carving, Norway, 1890. Collection of Vesterheim Norwegian-American Museum, Decorah, Iowa

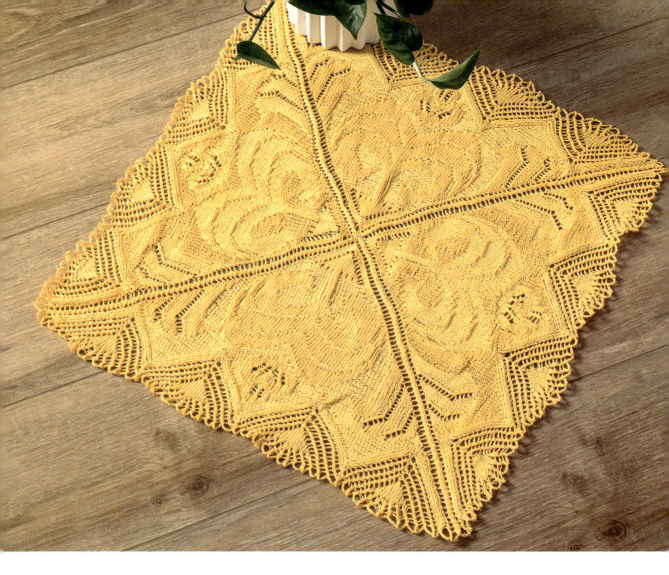

Notes

- The table cover is worked in the round from the center out and finished with a crochet bind-off.
- The table cover chart shows only odd-numbered rounds. See the chart key for even-numbered rounds. Charts A, B, and C show both odd and even rounds.
- I used a widely available cotton thread, Aunt Lydia's Crochet Thread Classic 10, which comes in many colors, so you can choose one that fits with your décor.

Stitch Guide

Crochet bind-off: Sl 2 sts (as indicated on chart) onto crochet hook, yo and draw through both sts. *Ch 6, sl next group of sts indicated on chart onto crochet hook, yo and draw through all sts; rep from * until no sts rem on needle. Ch 6, insert hook into top of first group of sts, yo and draw through all sts. Fasten off.

Instructions

With dpn, CO 8 sts. Place marker (pm) and join in the rnd. Next rnd [K2, pm] 3 times, k2. Work Rnds 1–138 of table cover chart, changing to shorter, then longer, cir needle when necessary—512 sts. Using the crochet method (see Stitch Guide), BO all sts.

Finishing

Weave in ends. Block, pinning out each chain loop in BO.

Figure 1. Lace Knitting Charts

Chart A

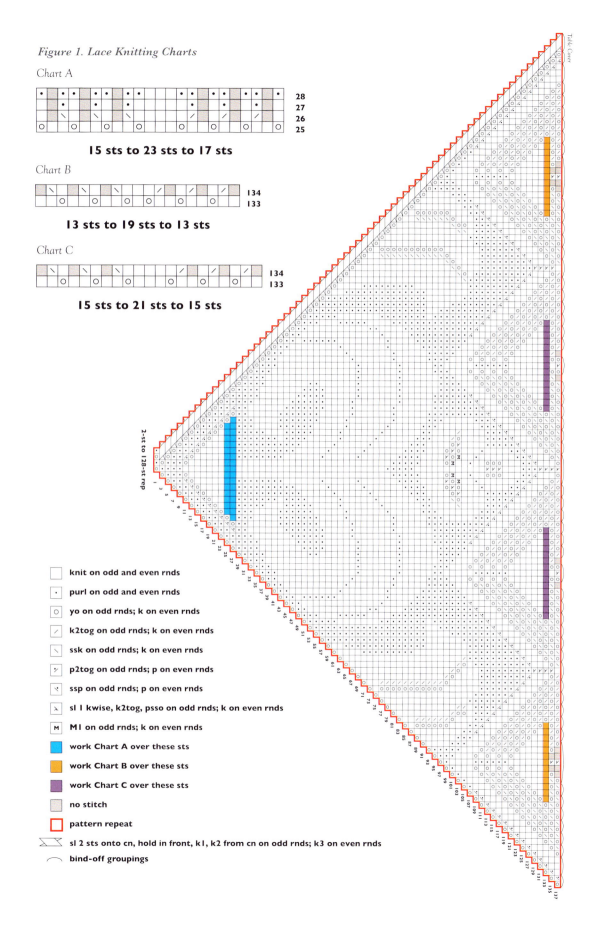

28
27
26
25

15 sts to 23 sts to 17 sts

Chart B

134
133

13 sts to 19 sts to 13 sts

Chart C

134
133

15 sts to 21 sts to 15 sts

□ knit on odd and even rnds

• purl on odd and even rnds

○ yo on odd rnds; k on even rnds

╱ k2tog on odd rnds; k on even rnds

╲ ssk on odd rnds; k on even rnds

⋎ p2tog on odd rnds; p on even rnds

⋏ ssp on odd rnds; p on even rnds

⅄ sl 1 kwise, k2tog, psso on odd rnds; k on even rnds

M M1 on odd rnds; k on even rnds

■ work Chart A over these sts

■ work Chart B over these sts

■ work Chart C over these sts

▨ no stitch

▢ pattern repeat

⧄ sl 2 sts onto cn, hold in front, k1, k2 from cn on odd rnds; k3 on even rnds

⌒ bind-off groupings

NORDIC FLOWERS TRAY HANGER

by JOHN MULLARKEY

CRAFT: *Weaving*

DIFFICULTY LEVEL: *Advanced beginner*

Band weaving in Scandinavia goes back to the Bronze Age, and tray hangers like this are also a Scandinavian tradition, often used to display prized copper trays or the rectangular tray used for serving almond cakes. This band is an original pattern inspired by Nordic designs as presented by Sonja Berlin in her book *Tablet Weaving in True Nordic Fashion.*[36] The pattern that caught my eye was a design with parallel fleur de lis, although she calls the pattern "cowberry." Using that as a guide, I developed my own take on that eight-color design.

Thread the cards using the included draft. Since I prefer using an inkle loom to support the warp, there is no way to work out twist as it builds up. This pattern as given in Berlin's book is turned in only a single direction, but as the twist builds up on an inkle loom, you will need to reverse the turning direction for all cards. For me that was after weaving every twelve fleur de lis. I think it adds a nice additional element to the design.

Structure: Warp-faced plain weave

Equipment
30 4-hole cards; belt shuttle; tension device (inkle loom; band loom, or warp can be tied to a door handle at one end and your belt at the other).

Materials
Yarns

Warp: 22/2 cottolin (3,200 yd/lb; Bockens; Glimakra USA), #2042 Light Green, 120 yd; #2017 Rust, 132 yd; #2001 White, 108 yd.

Weft: 22/2 cottolin, #2042 Light Green, 100 yd.

Other supplies: D-ring, 1½"; light green sewing thread; tapestry needle.

Warp Length

120 ends 3 yd (108") long (4 ends per card threaded in 30 4-hole cards).

Setts

Warp: n/a

Weft: About 20 ppi.

Dimensions
Band width: 1⅛".

Woven length: (measured under tension on the loom) About 84".

Finished size: (after washing, drying, and ironing) One band, 1⅛" wide by about 79" long.

Instructions

1. Wind a warp 3 yd long on your inkle loom. (If you're not using an inkle loom, you can wind a warp and set up the cards using the warping pegs for your rigid-heddle loom or a couple of large C-clamps spaced 3 yards apart.) Thread the warp ends through the tablets following the draft, figure 1. (See inset for threading instructions.)

2. Wind the belt shuttle with the weft yarn.

3. Align the tablets so that the D corners of the tablets are at the top front corner (front is toward you).

4. Begin weaving the strap, following the draft and being careful to maintain an even width. Leave a 4" tail on the first pick, then tuck that through the shed on the second pick to secure it. As you weave, turn the cards forward (away from you) for twelve flowers (48 picks), then back toward you for 12 flowers, and repeat until the piece measures about 79". On the last pick, before pressing in the previous pick with the belt shuttle, lay in the weft and then cut it, leaving a 6" tail. Thread the tail in the tapestry needle and use the needle to put it through the previous pick, leaving a loop at the selvedge. Press in the last pick with the belt shuttle, use the loop to snug in the last pick, and then pull the tail until the loop is gone.

5. Cut the band from the loom, leaving $^1/_2$" fringe at the ends.

6. Soak the strap in a basin of lukewarm water for about 30 minutes. Use a towel to press out excess moisture and lay it flat to dry. If needed, press with an iron on cotton setting.

7. To make the hanger, put the band through the D-ring and push the D-ring to the middle. Fold each half of the band back on itself, keeping it flat, and bring the end back through the D-ring underneath the center of the band and on the opposite side it exited from. Overlap the ends by about $^1/_2$", sew a seam across the bands next to each end, trim fringes, and you are ready to hang your plate or tray.

Figure 1. Flower Band Chart

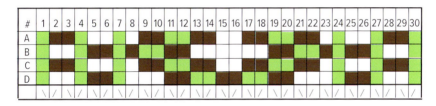

\ "S" threading. Threads enter cards from the printed (right) side of card

/ "Z" threading. Threads enter cards from the unprinted (left) side of card

Threading and Weaving from a Tablet Draft

If you haven't done tablet (card) weaving before, there are a few basics you'll need to know. First, and very important, notice that the cards are printed on only one side. As you work, all the cards should face the same direction. If you look at the photo of the threading in process on the inkle loom, you'll see that all the printed sides of the cards face to the weaver's right.

Second, you need to know how to understand the weaving draft. If you look at figure 1, you'll see numbers across the top that are the numbers of the cards. A lot of weavers like to number their cards in pencil to help them keep track of which card they're threading. There's also a column in the left side of the draft that says ABCD. These letters correspond to the letters on the card holes, and the colored rows to the right show what color should be threaded in each of these holes on each card. Along the bottom, you'll see lines that slant up to the left or the right. These tell you whether the threads should enter the card from the left side (the blank side in the set-up in the photo) or from the right side (the printed side in the photo). Tablet weavers also refer to these as an S-threading (threads entering from the right side of the card as you weave) or a Z-threading (threads entering from the left side of the card). If you look at the photo, you'll see that the first card on the right is threaded from the left side to the right, as the center bar of a letter Z is slanted, so this card has a Z-threading. (For this project, just make sure you alternate which side the cards are threaded from.)

Once your cards are set up and under tension, weaving is easy. Make sure the cards are all facing the same direction, with the D corner to the top front, as shown in the photo. To weave a pick, simply turn the cards all together a quarter turn away from you (forward) or toward you (backward) each pick, put in the weft pick, turn the cards another quarter turn, use the belt shuttle to snug down the previous pick, then lay in the next one. A quarter turn is moving the corners one position: for example, for the first forward pick, the D corner will move to the back top position and the A corner will move down and take the back bottom position. For this simple band, that's all there is to it!

Threading

S-threaded   **Z-threaded**

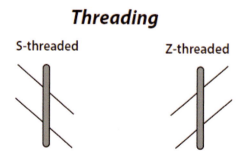

Figure 2. Threading Diagram

1. John's cards being threaded on the inkle loom.

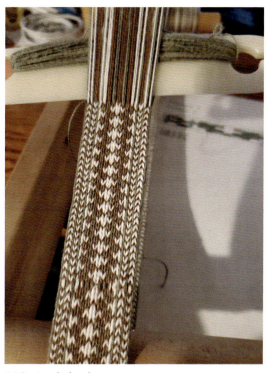

2. Weaving the band

3. Close-up of band in progress

A TAPESTRY TO TOTE

by LAURA BERLAGE

CRAFT: *Weaving*
DIFFICULTY LEVEL: *Advanced beginner*

Rutevev (Norwegian) or *rölakan* (Swedish) is a kind of geometric tapestry that has traditionally been used in Scandinavia for coverlets, cushion covers, or wall hangings.[37] It is also called "square weave," and the patterns do tend to be rectangles or stair-stepped diamonds made of squares, although traditional pieces also often include a jagged design called "lightning" (*lynild* in Norwegian or *viggrölakan* in Swedish). The weaving technique uses inter-locking wefts to avoid having slits, as you would find in a kilim tapestry or carpet.

This piece is inspired by a larger work by Karin Boe that was shown in *Selvedge* magazine in an article by Robbie LaFleur.

Structure: Geometric tapestry (weft-faced plain weave with weft interlock)

Equipment
Frame loom plus ¼" dowel 18" long **OR** rigid-heddle loom with an 8-dent heddle, 10" weaving width; pick-up stick (optional); tapestry beater or a heavy table fork.

Materials
Yarns

Warp: 12/6 cotton seine twine, also called *fiskgarn* (1,400 yd/lb; Bockens) or cotton carpet warp (1,600 yd/lb; 800 yd/8 oz cone; Maysville), Natural, 78 yd.

Weft: Any Aran weight 2-ply wool yarn (about 680 yd/lb), navy blue, 85 yd; black, 85 yd; red, 64 yd; yellow, 11 yd; light blue green, 11 yd. (Laura used yarn from her own business, Northstar Homestead. Harrisville Highland wool yarn and Brown Sheep Lamb's Pride are also good choices for this project.) Plus same yarn as weft, about 10 yd for headers.

Other supplies: Riavika Canvas Weekend Tote Bag (available on Amazon) or tote bag of your choice; coordinating sewing thread.

Warp Length

76 ends 18" or 1 yd long (depending whether you are using a rigid-heddle or frame loom; allows 18" for loom waste on a rigid-heddle loom).

Setts

Warp: 8 epi.

Weft: About 32 ppi.

Dimensions
Width in the heddle: 9⁴/₈".

Woven length: (measured under tension on the loom) About 11½".

Finished size: (tapestry only) 9½" by 10¾".

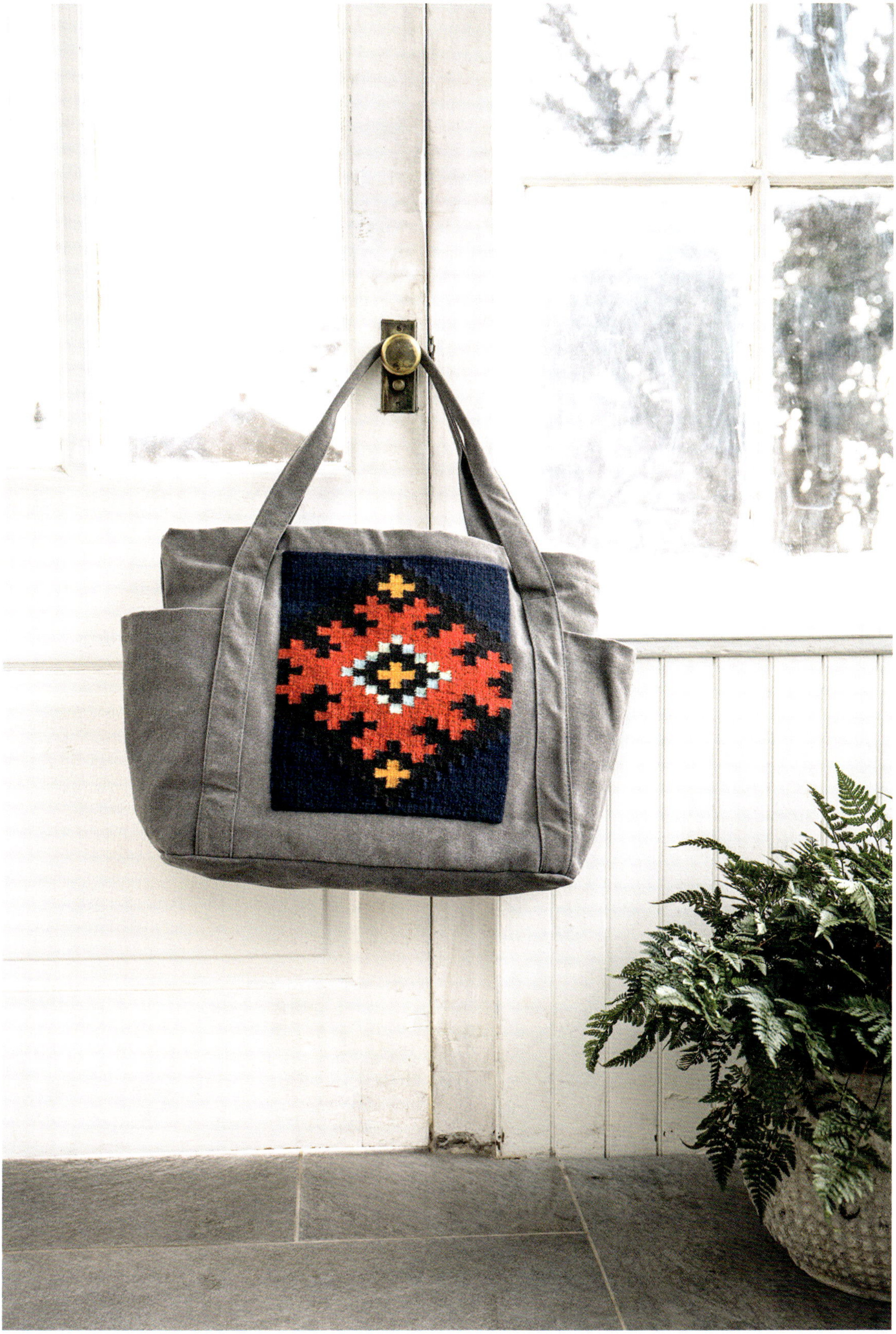

Top: Close-up of Karin Boe's design. Photo courtesy of Karen Boe.

Bottom: A classic example of *rutevev* (*rölaken*) with lynild (viggroläken) design. Stavanger Kunstmuseum, Stavanger, Norway. Photo by Veronna Capone.

Instructions

1. Warp your loom. For a rigid-heddle loom, set up your loom for direct warping a length of 36" or wind a warp of 76 ends 1 yd long, centering for a weaving width of 9⁴/₈". For a simple frame loom, warp in a figure-8 pattern, starting and ending at the bottom of the loom, 4 rounds per inch. Warp the piece to be 9.5 inches wide. When you weave the header, it will draw the front and back warps together, creating the 8 epi sett.

2. Wind butterflies of your weft yarns. (See inset.)

3. Weave a twined header to spread the warps evenly. (See figure 1.) After the first twined row, you can continue twining or weave plain weave until the header is about ³/₈".

4. Starting with the navy blue, weave 16 rows of plain weave the full width of the tapestry. (Use the rigid heddle for this or, if you're using a frame loom, you can use the pick-up stick to pick up every other warp and turn it on its side to make sheds.) Pound firmly with your beater or fork after each pick to pack the textile tightly. You should not see any warp threads showing in the woven area.

5. After the 16th row, begin weaving pattern. (You can refer to the Weaving the Interlock inset.) You won't use the pick-up stick or rigid heddle to make a shed as you weave the pattern, but you will continue alternating over-under or under-over each row as before. (We'll call these opposite sheds, even though you're not actually spreading the warp to make a shed opening.) Following the chart in figure 2, working left to right, lay in navy blue, going over and under the opposite warp threads from the pick before, for 36 warp ends, then leave the butterfly of yarn hanging. Lay in black yarn the same way for the next 4 warp threads and let the butterfly hang down. Finally, lay in navy blue on the last 36 warp threads and leave the butterfly hanging. Beat in the row with your beater. You've now worked your first pick of the pattern.

Figure 1. Twining a Header

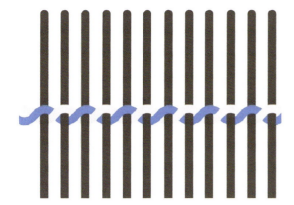

Figure 2. Rutevev Weaving Chart

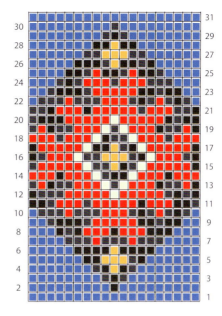

Each square represents 4 warp threads and 16 weft picks (8 turns).

To make a twined header, cut two lengths of the header yarn about 18" long or length needed for twining. Bring yarn 1 (gray in diagram) over the warp end on the right selvedge and yarn 2 (blue in diagram) under it. Cross yarn 1 in front of yarn 2 and bring it under the next warp end, then bring yarn 2 over the same warp end. Cross yarn 2 in front of yarn 1 and under next warp end, and bring yarn 1 over the same warp end. Repeat across.

If you want to continue twining another row, turn at the selvedge and bring the yarn that ended over the last warp end around and under it, and bring the one that ended underthe last warp end around and over it.

If you are twining only a couple of rows, you can begin with one longer length of the header yarn, fold in half, and secure with a lark's head knot around the first warp end at the selvedge, then begin twining across.

6. On the next row, starting at the right, weave the navy blue yarn back to the left for 36 warp threads, weaving in the opposite "shed" from the last row, then let the butterfly hang down. Pick up the black yarn, bring it up below and to the right of the hanging blue yarn to interlock, then weave to the left for 4 warp threads and drop the black yarn. Pick up the next navy blue yarn, catch the black yarn from as you did the black, and then weave it back to the left edge. Beat in the row.

7. Weave the next row in the opposite shed and with the same color sequence, working from left to right. Where the colors meet moving this direction, bring the new color up and to the left of the previous color to make the interlock.

8. Continue working this color sequence until you complete 16 rows to make a square, then begin working the next row of the chart the same way. The tapestry should look the same on both the front and the back of your piece. It should feel dense and firm, with no warps showing, and the sides should not be pulling inward. When you run out of a butterfly, always break instead of cutting the yarn. This will cause a tapered tail that you can lay into the shed and overlap with the new end so that the splice is invisible and there are no tails sticking out the back of the tapestry. When it is time to end a color, gently use a scissors in a scraping motion to feather the weft. You can wrap the next warp and lay it back into the same shed so that it ends nicely within the color section.

9. If, when working the single green squares, the pattern change moves the color one square to the right, you can carry the working yarn for that color to the right in the next row. If the pattern moves one square to the left, you will need to feather the weft over the old pattern section and then lay in your butterfly for the new pattern section. Jumping over to the new position without ending the weft in this case would leave an unsightly float on the front of the piece.

10. When you have finished weaving the design, work your second header as you did the first, ending with a row of twining.

11. Cut the tapestry from the loom, leaving several inches of warp at each end.

12. Tie the fringe with overhand knots in bundles of 3 (you'll have one bundle of 4), snugging them up against the header. and trim them to about 1" or your desired length if you plan to hang the tapestry.

13. Lightly steam the tapestry, if desired. Turn headers under and sew by hand onto a canvas tote bag, or just hang on a wall to admire.

Winding a Butterfly

The butterfly used for tapestry weaving is the same as you would use for stranded knitting. Simply put the end of a ball of yarn across your left palm and behind your thumb, leaving a tail. Bring the yarn over your thumb, across your palm, and behind your third finger, then back to and behind your thumb. Continue winding back and forth in a figure 8 until you have a comfortable amount of yarn wound into the butterfly. Take the butterfly off your left hand, pinching it in the center to hold it together. Break the working end of yarn from the ball, wrap it several times around the center of the butterfly, then tuck that end down through the wraps and tighten. The center wrap will keep the butterfly together, and the yarn will feed out of the butterfly starting with the tail you left at the beginning.

Winding a butterfly

Weaving Interlocking Tapestry

In this style of tapestry, you will lock the weft colors around each other each time they meet at a warp end. Here's how it works.

1. Working left to right, lay in first row of colors, in the opposite shed from the previous pick. (See photo **1**.) Note: to make things easy to see, these photos are showing just two colors. When you weave a tapestry, you will use the same process but with colors going all the way across the warp.

2. Bring the color on the right (in this case, red) around the warp end to its left and back to the left in the opposite shed. Let it hang in front of the weaving. (See photo **2**.)

3. Pick up the next color (in this case, gold), bring it up under the color to its right, and then weave it to the left in the opposite shed from the last gold pick. (See photo **3**.)

4. For the next row, pick up the right-hand color (red) and weaving back in the opposite shed from the last pick. (See photo **4**.) Then pick up the left-hand color and weave back. (See photo **5**.)

5. On the next row, change direction and repeat steps 2 and 3.

6. On the next row, repeat step 4.

7. Repeat this process until you complete a row of blocks in the design, then lay in new colors and start again.

1. Lay in the first pattern row, working left to right.

2. Change direction: weaving righthand color right to left.

3. Interlock weft and weave next color right to left.

4. Change direction: weave righthand color left to right.

5. Weave lefthand color left to right.

A CHEERFUL BAND OF MUG MATS

by SUSAN FOULKES

CRAFT: *Weaving*

DIFFICULTY LEVEL: *Advanced beginner*

I love weaving the narrow patterned bands that are used in so many ways throughout Scandinavia. They are traditionally used in so many ways: from decoration on folk costume to cradle ties, bag straps, and even adornments for the Indigenous Sámi people's reindeer. Now here is a lovely idea for you to use narrow woven bands creatively: colorful mug mats! It is also a great way to use up some of your band-weaving samples.

The mats (or mug rugs) are easy and fun to make with a little patience and a steam iron. My mats use two different striped bands: a Sámi band pattern in traditional colors, and the red, white, and blue striped band that is a Swedish pattern from Skåne.

For each mat, you'll weave two bands of the same width: a striped or patterned band and a plain-colored band for contrast. The pattern is written to give you two of each patterned band, and you can choose your contrast bands' colors.

The bands are very simple, with just two sheds and no pick-up or fancy patterning. You can weave them using an inkle loom or a bandle heddle (*grind*), which is just a miniature version of the heddle on your rigid-heddle loom.

Mug contents do spill occasionally, so these mug mats can be washed in a washing machine. They will shrink slightly but remain in shape. Another firm pressing brings them back into fine form. The mats look wonderful with the traditional Sámi carved wooden mugs.

Structure: Warp-faced plain weave

Equipment

Inkle loom, band loom, or small rigid-heddle loom; band heddle (optional); belt shuttle.

Materials

Yarns

Sámi-style Band

Warp: 22/2 cottolin (3,200 yd/lb; Bockens), #2064 Dark Green, 30 yd; #2066 Light Bright Red, 30 yd; #2029 Royal Blue, 24 yd; #2009 Light Yellow, 9 yd. **Weft:** 22/2 cottolin, #2064 Dark Green, 16 yd.

Swedish Band

Warp: 22/2 cottolin (3,200 yd/lb; Bockens), #2001 White, 54 yd; #2066 Light Bright Red, 36 yd; #2029 Royal Blue, 24 yd. **Weft:** 22/2 cottolin, #2001 White, 16 yd.

Solid Contrast Bands (for each band)

Warp: 22/2 cottolin (3,200 yd/lb; Bockens), #2001 White, #2066 Light Bright Red, #2029 Royal Blue, or #2009 Light Yellow, 48 yd per band. **Weft:** 22/2 cottolin, same color as band, 8 yd per band.

Other supplies: Iron; scissors; a 4" by 4" square of paper (card stock works well).

Warp Length

Sámi-style band: 31 ends 3 yd (108") long (makes 2 bands with extra length for tassels; allows 8" for take-up).

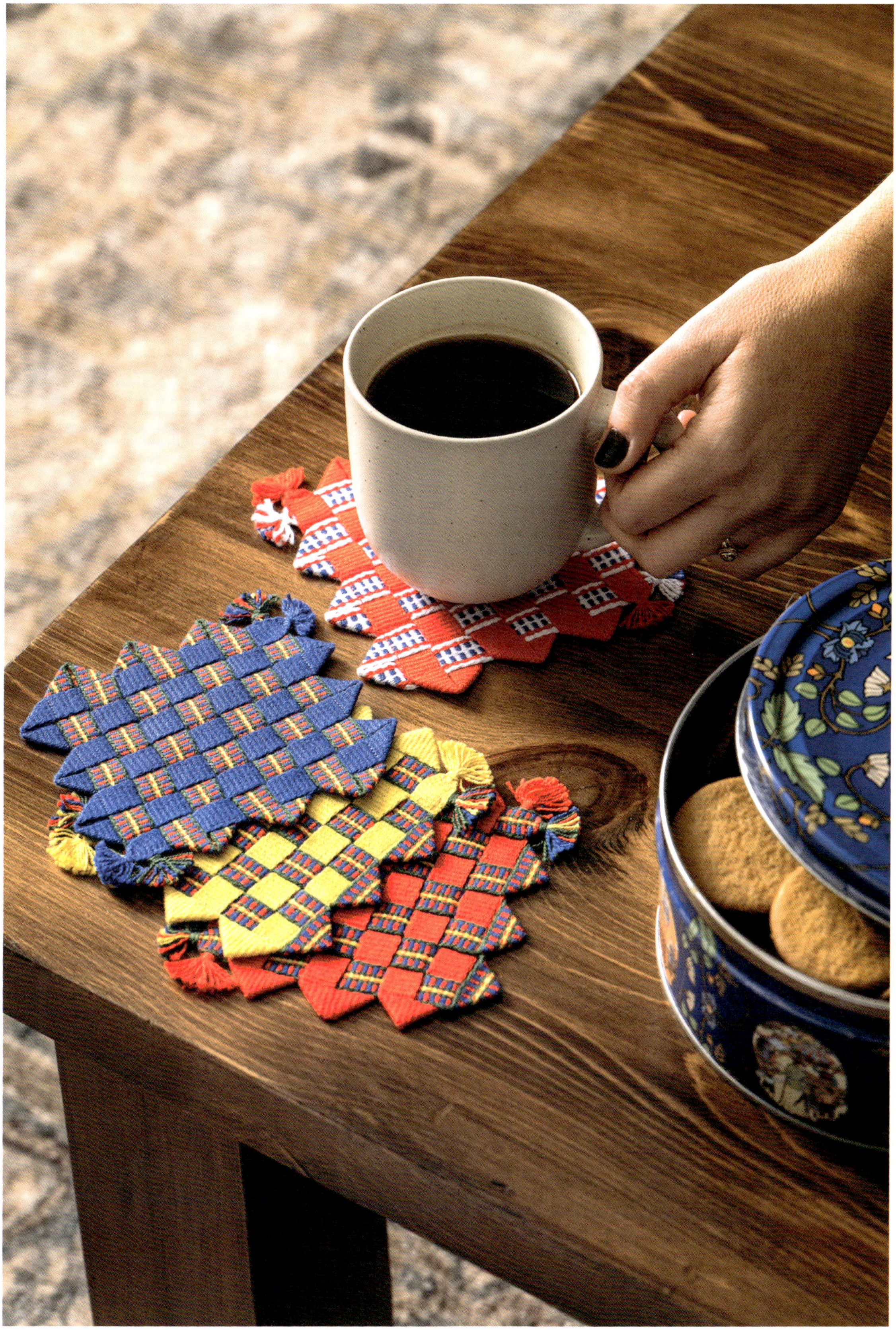

Swedish band: 33 ends 3 yd (108") long (makes 2 bands with extra length for tassels; allows 8" for take-up).

Solid-color bands (one band): 31 ends 54" long (makes 1 band with extra length for tassels; allows 4" for take-up; add 54" for each additional band in a color).

Setts

Warp: n/a

Weft: About 12 ppi.

Dimensions
Band width: ½".

Woven length: About 88" for two bands

Finished size: Four mug mats, 3½" by 3½".

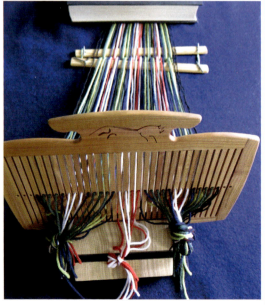

A band heddle, threaded and ready to weave. One end of the warp can be tied to a door or post, and the other can be tied to a belt at the weaver's waist.

Instructions

Weaving the bands:

1. For each patterned band, put a warp 3 yd long on your inkle loom or rigid-heddle loom, using the warp color charts in figure 1 and threading the warp through inkle heddles or a band heddle. (You can find my instructions for threading a band heddle here: durhamweaver64.blogspot.com/p/threading-heddle.html.)

2. Wind the belt shuttle with the weft yarn.

3. Weave one strap to 42", being careful to keep the bands to a consistent width. After the first band, skip 4" of warp and weave a second band 40" long. Remove the band from the loom, leaving a few inches of fringe at each end.

4. Weave two bands in the other pattern the same way.

5. Weave 4 solid-color bands in whatever colors you prefer.

6. Wash all bands by soaking in a basin for ½ hour or so in warm water. They will be about ½" wide and about 40" long after washing. This gives you enough length to weave the mats and make the tassels at each end.

Weaving the mug mats:

1. Cut out a 4" by 4" square of paper or card. This is now the template for the first band. (For this mug mat, both bands are approximately ½" wide. There are seven woven "rounds" of each band for the mug mat, so if your bands are a different width, multiply the width by 7 and add ½" to allow for the contrasting band to be woven over and under the striped band. Cut your paper square to that size.)

2. Lay the band down the length of the template, fold it as shown in photo **1**, and iron the fold firmly, making a nice point. Take the band up and parallel to the first strip and again fold and iron firmly.

3. Continue folding and pressing until you have 7 lengths of the striped band laid out, covering the paper square.

4. Start weaving the solid-color band over and under the striped band. At each turn, iron the fold firmly, making a neat point. Keep going until seven rounds are completed. The last strip has to be eased into position by adjusting the other strips to make room. Once the mug mat is woven, it can be pressed flat. (See photos **2** and **3**.)

5. Sew around the edges to ensure stability, using a straight stitch and thread that matches the solid-color band. The mug mat will now be firm and stable.

6. Make the end tassels: Unravel the weft in the band ends sticking out of the mat, keeping the weft attached. Unravel down to the edge of the mat, then pull the weft firmly to gather the end of the band as much as possible. Next, take about 12" of cottolin in the edge color of the band, Put the center of this thread under the base of the tassel and tie around the tassel with a half-knot (half of a square knot). Turn the mat over and tie another half-knot. (See photo **4**.) Repeat until you've tied five half-knots, then turn over one last time (to the back) and tie a square knot. Press firmly and the knot will flatten. (This is known as West Country whipping, and you can find good videos on YouTube if you want to see it done.) Smooth the ends of the tie thread into the tassel.

7. Bind each band end the same way. Once all the tassels are made and pressed flat, trim them to about ½" long. Your mug mat is now complete.

Figure 1. Threading Charts

Swedish-style Band

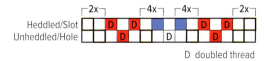

Sami-style Band

Bands may be woven with band heddle or on inkle loom.
For inkle loom. read drafts from left to right, as they are threaded.

1. The folding process

2. Weaving the two bands together

3. Press and stitch   4. Making the end tassels

CHAPTER FIVE

THE BEAUTY OF SUSTAINABILITY

That which leaves no trace has done no harm.

—*Icelandic proverb*

The Nordic countries have earned an international reputation for sustainability and environmental innovation. In 2019, the Nordic Council of Ministers also announced their shared vision to become the world's most sustainable and integrated region by 2030, promoting a green, competitive, and socially sustainable Nordic region. The member countries are actively investing in low-carbon infrastructure and no-waste practices. And other countries are noticing: a US ad during the 2022 Super Bowl featured comedian Will Farrell declaring, "We're coming for you, Norway," challenging Norway's superiority in electric-car ownership per capita.[38] But how has Scandinavia earned its reputation for sustainability?

SUSTAINABILITY AS REALISM

The Scandinavian culture of sustainability is not just branding. It is firmly based in realism. There is an old Norwegian saying: "The water is the same on both sides of the boat." Scandinavians understand that what affects one affects us all. With their shared experience of scarcity and the fearsome power of nature, they know that the threats of climate change, pollution, and resource depletion are genuine and impending.

Certainly, over the last two centuries the Scandinavian countries have made many of the same economic and environmental trade-offs as other countries.

Since the late nineteenth century, farming, mining, and tourism have disrupted the lives of the Indigenous Sámi and exploited the resources of Sápmi, their traditional migration range in northern Norway, Sweden, Finland, and Russia. Norway's current prosperity is based on North Sea oil. And the Baltic ecosystem has been threatened by farm runoff from Sweden and overfishing by Denmark. But, contradictions aside, the Nordic nations are sincerely committed to sustainability.

Because climate change is affecting the polar regions even faster than other parts of the planet, the Nordic countries are tackling the issues and challenging the rest of the world to join them. In Norway, 98% of electrical production comes from renewable resources. Sweden has built infrastructure for electric-car charging and offered solar energy grants to its communities, and since 2011, less than 1% of Swedish household waste has gone to landfills. Since 1996, Denmark has successfully cut its CO_2 emissions by more than half, and about half of its electricity comes from wind power. Denmark also led the EU in banning the export of hazardous waste to the developing world. Finland was the first country in the world to develop a road map for the efficient and sustainable use of resources, and Iceland meets 100% of its electricity and heating needs through hydropower and geothermal energy. But sustainability runs deeper than just public policy in Nordic countries, as we shall soon see.

SUSTAINABILITY AS TRADITION

Living in harmony with the land is ingrained into Scandinavian culture, a part of what the Swedes would call *folkvett*, or common sense. With its thin soil, sparse arable land, and fleeting warmth and sunlight, the Nordic region was never going to be a land of plenty. Over millennia, its peoples have adapted to scarcity, coaxing crops out of tiny farms carved from forests, mountainsides, and the shores of fjords. Farmers with access to trees had to supplement their

incomes with the hard work of timber harvesting, but the forests of Scandinavia are not like the towering forests I grew up with in the Pacific Northwest, nurtured by our rich volcanic soil. When my cousin Kristian first visited from Norway, he marveled at our tall trees, and when I went to Scandinavia, I marveled at the sparse, open forests of trees, which were diminutive compared to the ones I knew. A farmer's timber would have grown slowly in the old country, and he would have needed more trees to build a home or barn.

Even the resources that were abundant in the North came with a price. Fisherman braved the stormy Baltic and North Sea for fish to eat and trade, and miners toiled in the unforgiving mountains for iron ore, silver, and gold.

Perhaps the most precious resource was time: the short summers to prepare for another winter; the many demands of crop raising, herding animals, and producing implements, textiles, and household items. Common sense was the key to survival. Wherever possible, needs were met with the materials at hand: wood and wool, leather and straw, iron and stone. Each season had its tasks, and they were combined when possible. A girl could knit as she tended the herds in the summer pasture. A mother could weave bands for garters or reins as she waited for a pot to boil. A man could whittle a spoon or bowl as he waited for fish to bite. The power of nature was also harnessed. A water-driven *stampa*, or fulling mill, turned a community's woven cloth into *vadmal*, sturdy felted material used for garments since the Viking Age. Felled trees could be slid down a snowy chute, then floated down a river for sale. No season, no material, and no effort was wasted.

SUSTAINABLE ARCHITECTURE, THEN AND NOW

When the storms of winter howled overhead, the ancestors of today's Scandinavians knew how to keep snug. Since before the Vikings, people in many areas built turf-roofed houses, using the earth itself to protect them. The roof timbers of a log home would be covered in birch bark, then laid with sections of sod. The birch bark made the roof waterproof, and the thick sod would hold the bark in place, provide insulation, and weight down the log walls, pushing the logs together and helping to prevent drafts. In Iceland, a whole structure might be turfed: the

buildings were recessed slightly into the ground, then foundations of stone were laid, topped by wooden walls or frames to hold sections of turf, and more turf would be laid on the roof. These sturdy living walls and ceilings would absorb moisture and insulate the interior, with minimal upkeep required. I've seen turf-roofed homes in central Sweden, and in Iceland, many of these *torfbæir* have survived to this day.

Rural people also took advantage of the prevailing weather and available materials to store food for the winter. The *stabbur* or storehouse was built of logs, raised up on posts that were topped with slabs of stone to keep mice from crawling in to eat or nest in the supplies. To further deter the mice, the steps up to the stabbur ended enough short of the entrance that rodents couldn't jump the gap. If a stabbur had windows, they were small, to keep the inside cool during the summer and warm enough during the winter. Grain, preserved meat, cheese and butter, and some textiles could be kept safely through to the next season.

Modern Nordic architecture carries on these traditions. Contemporary public buildings fit the structure to the environment and intended use, choosing simple lines to withstand storms and snowloads, taking advantage of natural materials and available light, and building in sustainability. Like a stabbur, the University of Copenhagen's Green Light House, Denmark's first carbon-neutral public building, is heavily insulated and stores excess heat and cold to efficiently regulate the inside temperature, although its atrium fills it with light. The Sametinget, the Sámi Parliament building of Norway, built in the shape of the traditional *lavvu*, a reindeer-hide tent, uses natural materials and is filled with natural light. Contemporary homes, too, are made to blend with the environment, with neutral colors and wood inside and out, simple shapes built to last, cozy living spaces, and open layouts to let the available light into every corner.

Stabbur at the Bygdetun, museum, Telemark, Norway. Photo in the collection of the Norwegian Directorate for Cultural Heritage.

SUSTAINABILITY AS ART AND CRAFT

Scarcity and the attendant need for efficiency also shaped Nordic arts and crafts. Homes, textiles, and furniture all were made to last. And because they would last, they deserved to be beautiful, from the hinge on a door to the handle of a wooden spoon. People were able to create vibrant designs based on nature for themselves, using simple tools.

In *The Red Thread*, the editor observes that "[the Nordic] reliance on the land also had an integral effect on its design culture. If they built a house, it had to be able to stand for generations, and the furniture passed down with it. Personal possessions and decorations were minimal, therefore, and a cherished cup, knife, or blanket was an object for your children and grandchildren to inherit."[39] So, house, furniture, cup, and blanket were made with care and beauty, gifts to the generations to come.

A Seat for the Ages: The Kubbestol

The *kubbestol* (Norwegian) or *kubbstol* (Swedish) is the ultimate example of furniture made from natural material to be handed down. "Kubb" refers to the 3-or-4-foot section of tree trunk from which the chair is carved. According to Janice Stewart, these chairs, are mentioned in the Nordic sagas, but were not common in households until the mid-eighteenth century, perhaps because they reminded people of a throne.[40] In fact, a Viking Age carving from Sanda churchyard in Gotland, Sweden, depicts what are thought to be the Norse gods Odin and Frigg sitting on kubbestols.

From the mid-seventeenth to the mid-twentiethth centuries, *kubbestole/kubbstolar* carved from logs were common in rural areas along the border between Norway and Sweden. (The Danish version of a kubbestol is made more like a barrel, with staves for the legs and back.) Originally, the kubbestol would have been be reserved for the head of the household, although a wealthy farm might boast more than one kubbestol. By the mid-1800s, there are even examples of child-sized kubbestols. They were often decorated with elaborate carving or painting, or both, and old chairs with layers of decorative painting to suit the current style show that they were handed down for generations.

Kubbestol making has been revived today by American carvers working in the Nordic tradition, and I personally hope they catch on. They are a beautiful, long-lasting use of natural material, and I love the way they marry practicality and beauty. In fact, I could only laugh and agree with the author of a design blog who examined the theory that the kubbestol originated in Etruscan funerary practices. He discarded it because "the *kubbestol/kubbstol* has such an inherent logic, is so obviously how you would make a chair if you didn't know how to make a chair but had a tree, that we can see no way past some unrecorded, and chairless, (proto-) Scandinavian standing in front of a tree and thinking, 'What if . . .'"[41]

A Tradition of "Slow Cloth"

Manufactured cloth was a major impetus of the Industrial Revolution, and it has been a mixed blessing from the start, from inhumane working conditions in the early mills to the environmental hazards of industrial cotton and linen production, dyestuffs released in the environment, and today's consumer culture of throwaway clothing that ends up in landfills. Two movements have arisen in reaction to these ills: the "fibershed" concept of using locally produced materials, and a call for hand-produced "slow cloth."

Swedish tapestry artist Helena Hernmarck has said that Scandinavians can be thankful the Industrial Revolution came late to the North, and so the tradition of handmade cloth was not lost or devalued as it was elsewhere in Europe and America. For centuries, a large part of rural Scandinavian life was dedicated to cloth production: raising sheep and flax, processing and spinning the fiber, knitting garments, and weaving cloth for clothing and household textiles. Scandinavia also has its own history of commercial cloth production, of course. By the end of the Viking period, the Icelanders were sending wool cloth and *gråfellar*, rya cloaks or throws that used locks of gray Icelandic fleece for the pile, to mainland Scandinavia in exchange for trade goods. By the early eighteenth century, specialized Swedish weavers were producing linen damask textiles for the royal house and nobles, and Sweden's first

Left: The Gotland runestone. The figures at the top, thought to represent the gods Odin and Frigg, are seated on kubbestols. Photo by Berig.

Right: Kubbestol carved from a single piece of wood, decorated with fine acanthus carving. Made by Halvor Lie, Kristiansand, Norway. ca. 1900. The tree trunk used to make this chair grew in a forest on the coast west of Kristiansand. The piece of wood was so heavy that the horse wagon used to transport it broke. Collection of Vesterheim Norwegian-American Museum, Decorah, Iowa.

Left: Restored Jacquard loom, Hørvævsmuseet (The Flax Weaving Museum), Glamsbjerg, Denmark. Photo by Veronna Capone.

Right: My favorite Fjällraven *kånken*, made with recycled wool: Sweden's eco-friendly fashion answer to the Prada backpack.

mechanical cotton-weaving mill was established outside Borås in 1835. But just as industrialization brought mass-produced textiles to Scandinavia, the National Romantic movement elevated the folk arts, so they were preserved through newly founded folk schools and handcraft organizations.

Like other aspects of Nordic industry, textile production is now being refocused on sustainability. The Nordic Council's textile strategy calls for a "closed-loop" textile lifecycle,[42] and textile designers and producers throughout Scandinavia are now promoting "circular fashion": making garments to last longer, offering discounts for the return of old clothing, offering repair services, and sourcing materials from local farmers. Sustainably produced textiles are also popular with Nordic consumers, including those that are handmade using traditional techniques and materials.

RAGS-TO-RICHES RUG

by TOM KNISELY

CRAFT: *Weaving*

DIFFICULTY LEVEL: *Advanced beginner*

When someone mentions rag rugs, do you think of a rustic kitchen or cabin? Do you think about recycling cloth? I'll bet you don't think "status symbol." But in Scandinavia, that's exactly how rag rugs started out: as a status symbol.

For centuries, cloth production required long hours and hard labor, so textiles were mended and passed down. When they were too worn to mend, they became patches for other clothing, blankets, etc. When they were too worn to patch, they were sold to the rag merchant to be turned into paper. No one would have used precious rags for floor coverings.

But in the mid-nineteenth century, industrialization brought factory-made fabric and a growing middle class eager to travel and to furnish their homes in popular European fashion. On their travels, they saw rag rugs, a luxury that was, at first, set out on the floor only for special occasions. Over time, the trend spread to rural areas, where people now had wooden floors instead of the packed-earth floors that had been common for centuries. By then, paper was made from wood pulp, so there was no rag merchant to buy discarded textiles, and weaving rag rugs made financial sense. Rag rugs were also great for warmth, and they were practical because they could be taken outside to beat the dust off or washed in summer, making them much easier to clean than heavy wool rugs.

Structure: Plain weave

Equipment

Rigid-heddle loom, 24" weaving width; 8-dent heddle; 2–4 stick shuttles; thin-edged pick-up stick longer than 24" bundles.

Materials

Yarns

Warp: 12/6 cotton seine twine, also called *fiskgarn* (1,400 yd/lb; Bockens), Natural, 500 yd.

Weft: 12/6 cotton seine twine, 6 yd. Four different flannel fabrics, cut into ¾"-wide strips. Fabric A, 88 yd; Fabrics B and D, 54 yd; Fabric C, 36 yd.

Warp Length

200 ends 2½ yd (90") long (includes 4 doubled ends at each selvedge; allows 8" for take-up, 28" for loom waste; loom waste includes fringe).

Setts

Warp: 8 epi.

Weft: About 7 ppi.

Dimensions

Width in the heddle: 24".

Woven length: (measured under tension on the loom) 54".

Finished size: 22¾" by 52" plus fringe.

Figure 1. Weft Color Order

Numbers indicate picks of that color unless followed by the inch symbol ("). In that case, weave that color for as many inches as indicated.

Instructions

1. Set up your loom for direct warping a length of 90" or wind a warp of 200 ends 2½ yd long. Warp the loom using your preferred method, centering for a weaving width of 24" and doubling the first 4 warp ends and the last 4 warp ends.

2. Spread the warp with scrap yarn, allowing at least 6" for fringe. Wind a 3 yards of the cotton seine twine on one of your stick shuttles, then weave 4 picks to make a header for the rug. Tuck in tails on the second and last pick.

3. Wind stick shuttles with the flannel fabrics and weave the rug, following the weft color order in figure 1. Use the rigid-heddle to push the rag weft into place, then, when you open the next shed, use the pick-up stick to really pack it down before inserting the next pick. When you change fabric colors, leave a 6" tail of the fabric you're finishing, cut it to taper the width, and tuck it into the next shed. Taper the end of the new fabric color and lay it against the tail of the old color.

4. When you complete the color order, weave 4 more picks with seine twine, then weave a few picks with scrap yarn to protect the end.

5. Remove your fabric from the loom, leaving at least 6" of warp at each end for fringes.

6. Removing the scrap yarn a little at a time, tie the fringe with overhand knots snug against the headings, in bundles of 4 ends. Cut the bundles to about 3" long. (I like to lay them all flat on a self-healing cutting mat, smooth them out, and then cut with a rotary cutter so that they come out nice and even.)

7. Machine wash your rug on a gentle cycle in warm water, then hanging to dry.

8. Place on your floor (with a rug pad if your floor is slippery), snuggle your toes in, and enjoy!

Preparing Rags

If you read Scandinavian weaving books or magazines today, you will undoubtedly find patterns for rag rugs. They are still a great way to recycle (and, I would say, to upcycle) fabrics, from old, worn jeans to old sheets. This rug is made with flannel, some of it the kind you'd use for flannel shirts or jackets, and some of it sheet/pillowcase fabric. If you can't find enough in your closets or at your local thrift store, you can also find flannel remnants on clearance at the fabric store. When you're shopping, don't worry about whether you like the pattern. Instead, squish the cloth in your hand and see if you like the color. That's what will show in your rug. As a guideline, you'll need about 1 square yard of fabric for every square foot of rug.

Tearing fabric into rags is a lot of fun, especially if you do it with a friend. If it's a remnant, wash it first. Then make cuts every ¾" along the edge, several inches deep. Next, you and your friend take turns grabbing every other cut tab and adding them to a bundle in your hand. Once they're all bundled, hold tight, step back, and let 'er rip! It's quick and easy, and it will make you laugh.

The fabrics that Tom used for his rag rug.

TOWELS TO TREASURE

by ANITA OSTERHAUG

CRAFT: *Weaving*

DIFFICULTY LEVEL: *Advanced beginner*

One of the questions I would sometimes pose to readers when I was editor of *Handwoven* magazine was "Why does it matter that we weave a towel?" We can buy perfectly good cloth towels at the store. I've bought commercially woven kitchen towels that are both attractive and inexpensive. And, of course, there are paper towels.

But I think it does matter that we weave our own towels. As I traveled and saw beautiful handmade textiles in Scandinavian folk schools and homes, I realized that a handwoven towel makes everything that happens in your kitchen a little more special. It will often be more absorbent than commercially made towels, it will wear far better, and, best of all, you won't throw it away. Instead, it will be something that you treasure for years and years, and it will grow softer and more beautiful with each washing.

The cottolin yarn in these towels is used doubled in both warp and weft. The alternating greens allow you to change from making vertical to horizontal stripes, and the pink is just to give the towels a hint of spring. You can weave the stripes as I have, or have fun making up your own stripe sequences. Like the monk's belt guest towels in chapter 3, you can weave these in different colors for different seasons or weave them in your friends' favorite colors and give them as gifts.

Structure: Plain weave

Equipment
Rigid-heddle loom, 18" weaving width; 10-dent reed; 3 stick shuttles; pick-up stick; tapestry needle for weaving in ends.

Materials
Yarns

Warp: 22/2 cottolin, used doubled (3,200 yd/lb; Bockens; Glimakra USA), #2062 Olive Gold, 344 yd; #2041 Pastel Yellow Green 264 yd; #2051 Pink, 76 yd.

Weft: 22/2 cottolin, used doubled, #2062 Olive Gold, 360 yd; #2041 Pastel Yellow Green 300 yd; #2051 Pink, 50 yd.

Warp Length

171 ends 2 yd (72") long (warp yarn is used doubled; allows 5" for take-up, 19" for loom waste).

Setts

Warp: 10 epi.

Weft: About 14 ppi on towel body, about 20 ppi for hems.

Dimensions
Width in the reed: 17$\frac{1}{10}$" in a 10-dent reed.

Woven length: (measured under tension on the loom) 48".

Finished size: (after wet-finishing and hemming) Two towels, 14" by 21".

Figure 1. Warp Color Order

	7x	4x	7x	3x	7x	2x	2x	2x	2x	7x	3x	7x	4x	8x	
19		1		1		1	1		1		1		1		◻ Pink
66	1	1		1	1		1	1		1	1		1	1	◻ Pastel Yellow Green
86	1	1	1	1	1	1	1	1	1	1	1	1	1	1	◻ Olive Gold

171 ends total

Instructions

1. Set up your loom for direct warping a length of 72" or wind a warp of 171 ends 2 yd long, following the warp color order in figure 1. Remember that the cottolin is used doubled. If you're direct warping, you can alternate putting a loop of the darker green through each slot and a loop of the lighter green or the pink through each hole. If you're winding on a warping board, you can hold the two greens together, separated by your finger to keep tension, then, instead of cutting the ends, simply put a loop through each hole and slot, leaving open holes for the pink threads, then add those later. Warp the loom, starting and ending in a slot and centering for a weaving width of 17¹⁄₁₀".

2. Spread the warp with scrap yarn. I suggest using something woolen and a little fuzzy, such as scraps of Lopi. This will stay in place to protect the end once you have the fabric off the loom.

3. Wind a stick shuttle with about 10 yd of single Olive Gold (which is actually olive green) and weave ³⁄₄" with the single weft. This will be turned under for the hem.

4. Wind one stick shuttle with doubled cottolin in each of the three colors. This will be easiest if you wind balls of the yarn and then wind the balls together onto the stick shuttle, using your fingers to maintain even tension on the strands.

5. Starting with the rigid heddle in the up position, weave the first towel according to the color sequence shown in figure 2. You don't have to pack the weft in too hard. Go for a fairly balanced weave; the length will shrink some when the fabric is off the loom. When you complete the color sequence, weave another ³⁄₄" with the single weft,

Figure 2. Weft Color Order

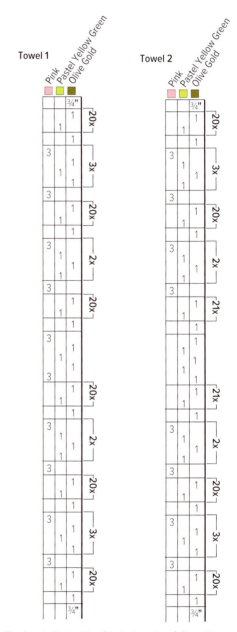

Numbers indicate picks of that color unless followed by the inch symbol ("). In that case, weave that color for as many inches as indicated.

¾" hems on towels are woven with a single thread of Olive Green. All other areas are woven with doubled threads of all the colors.

put in a few picks of scrap yarn to separate the towels, then weave the second towel as you did the first, weaving $3/4$" for hem at each end and following the other color order in figure 2. Finish by weaving a few more picks of scrap yarn.

6. Cut the fabric from the loom, leaving the scrap yarn in place to protect the ends.

7. Machine wash the fabric in warm water, dry, and press with iron on the cotton setting.

8. Remove the scrap yarn. Fold the ends in about $1/4$", iron, then fold under $1/2$" again, iron, and handsew hems to the back side.

9. Iron hems, and your towels are ready to use.

Towel-Hanging Tabs
by Becky Ashenden

Handwoven kitchen towels are satisfyingly pretty when folded and hanging over a towel bar, but towels are made to be used. One of the very practical features that Scandinavians expect in a kitchen towel is a little tab on a back corner, so that you can quickly hang it on a hook after

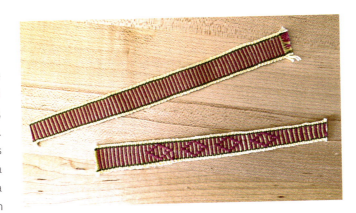

using it. If you've bought towels from IKEA, for example, you've probably noticed and made use of those handy tabs. For my towels, Becky Ashenden, owner and teacher at Vävstuga Weaving School in Massachusetts, wove these pretty hanging tabs, so I've included the pattern in case you want to make some too. You could weave these on an inkle loom, a rigid-heddle loom, or a band loom. Becky wove them on a band loom that she designed for Vävstuga, basically a tall inkle loom that you can sit at comfortably and that can accommodate long warps.

Figure 1. Charts for Woven Tabs

Diamond Pick-up

Band Threading

Bands may be woven with band heddle or on inkle loom. For inkle loom. read drafts from left to right, as they are threaded.

For striped band, simply alternate sheds. For diamond band, alternately pick up 3 Magenta threads and drop corresponding Citrine threads on down/push sheds as shown in pick-up chart. Each outlined square represents 3 Magenta threads picked up.

WHY KNOT? MARKET BAG

by ANITA OSTERHAUG

CRAFT: *Knitting*

DIFFICULTY LEVEL: *Intermediate*

One of the things that impressed me from my very first travels in Europe was that Europeans, including Scandinavians, brought nice woven or knotted bags with them when they went shopping. Even if a store supplied a bag, it was most likely to be paper. Throwaway plastic bags were rarely seen.

Fast-forward to today: our environment and oceans are filling with throwaway plastic bags. People in America are now encouraged to bring their own bags when shopping, so we often use sturdy reusable woven plastic or microfiber ones. And reusable is important, but the bags I see still lack the charm of the bags that Scandinavians have used probably for as long as people have been going to market.

I designed this little market bag in the colors of spring, to bring a bit of Scandinavian prettiness to your shopping experience. I first thought about weaving a bag in *krokbragd*, a technique used in traditional coverlets and, more recently, rugs. But woven krokbragd is heavy, and, besides, the patterning is so pretty and versatile, why should weavers have all the fun? So, here you have it: knitted krokbragd. Because, why (k)not?

Structure: Stranded knitting

Materials

Yarn Lily Sugar 'n Cream "Super Size" (100% cotton; 190 yd [174 m] / 4 oz [113 g]):

>   **MC:** Teal, 2 balls (allows enough for optional finger-woven strap)
>
>   **CC1:** Hot Pink, 1 ball
>
>   **CC2:** Key Lime Pie Ombre, 1 ball
>
>   **CC3:** Hot Orange, 1 ball
>
>   **CC4:** Mod Blue, 1 ball

Needles Size 7 (4.5 mm): 24" circular (cir). Adjust needle size if necessary to obtain the correct gauge.

Notions Markers (m); tapestry needle; one spare needle in same size or smaller for "Magic Circle" Start; 2½ yd long purchased or woven strap; sewing thread to match MC; straight pins; contrasting embroidery thread; sewing machine.

Gauge 23 sts and 24 rnds = 4" in stranded St st.

Dimensions
Finished Size: 17" tall by 15" wide.

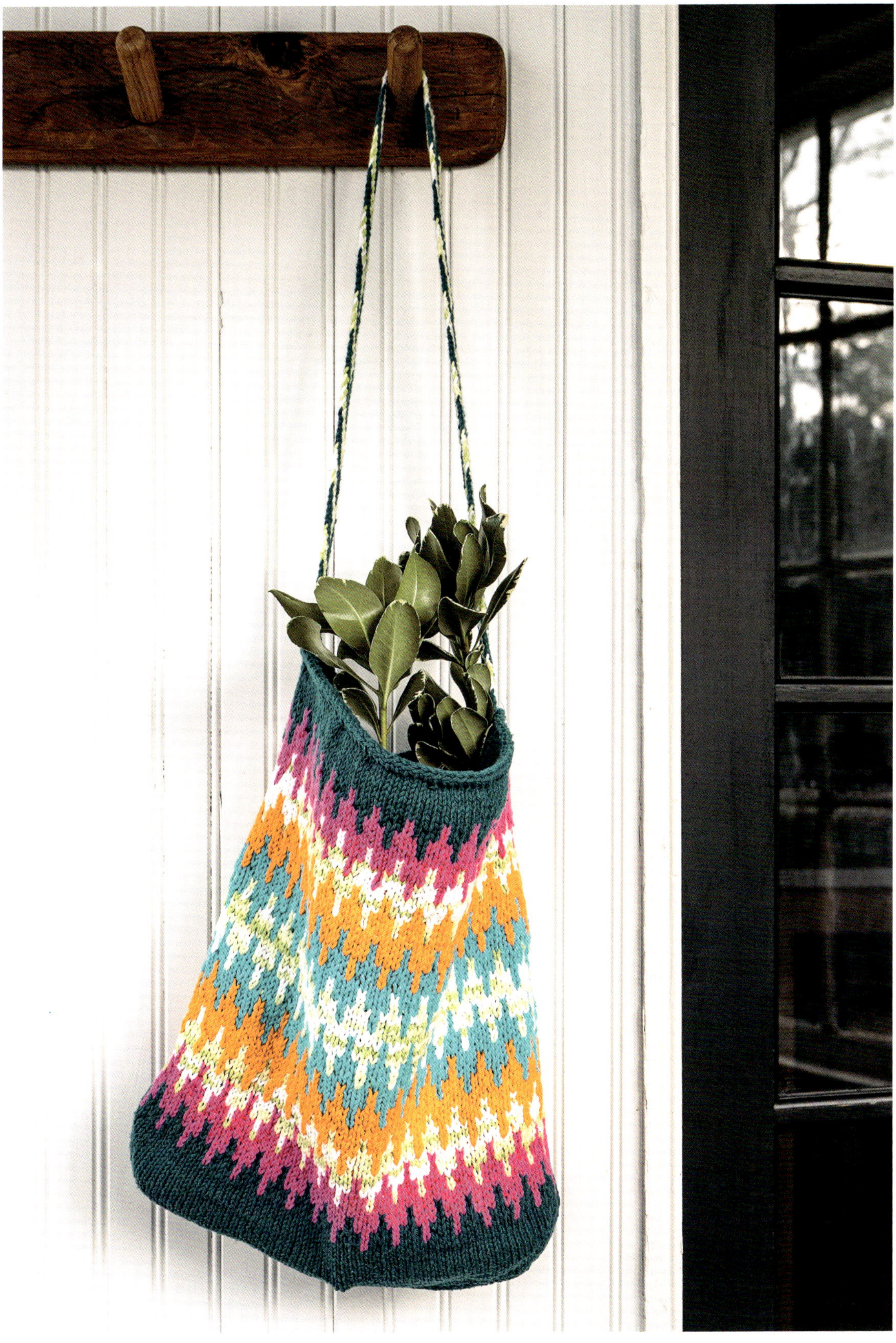

The bag is made with Lily Sugar 'n Cream cotton yarn, which comes in oodles of pretty colors and is available in many craft stores and online. It's inexpensive, wears well, and is washable. The bag is strong because of the carried yarn on the inside and because the strap is sewn to the inside all the way down the sides and across the bottom.

You can buy a coordinating strap for your bag at the fabric store, or you can weave your own, as I did (see the next project). I didn't line my bag, but if you want to use yours for heavy items or as a project bag for knitting, for instance, you might choose to line it.

Notes

- The bag is knitted in the round, but it doesn't start out that way. The starting technique for this project is one I learned from Norwegian knitting historian, teacher, and recipient of the King's Order of Merit, Annemor Sundbø. (Yes, Scandinavian knitters get more respect!) In a class called "Magical Knitting," Annemor taught us to cast on one row of stitches and turn it into a circle, a handy trick for many things, including knitting magical creatures. (I knitted a very toothy troll in the class.) I used this technique to start the bag because it gives a nice, firm bottom seam.
- The flexible bind-off allows the bag opening to stretch a bit so that you can put things inside it easily, but the decreases in the row before the bind-off keep it from flopping open and spilling its contents.
- Tension: The cotton yarn has very little stretch to it, so avoid knitting tightly except on the first 4 rows. If you knit tightly, your bag will turn into Viking armor for your groceries.
- Carrying colors: The floats in this stranded knitting pattern are never more than 3 stitches, so it is not necessary to catch the floats with the working yarn. Be sure to stretch the work as you go to keep the floats loose, and keep the working yarn loose if you do choose to catch the floats.

Stitch Guide

"Magic circle" start: Row 1 (WS): *K1f&b; rep from * to end—st count is doubled.

Rows 2 and 3: *K1, sl 1 pwise wyf; rep from * to end, pulling the knit sts tog firmly.

Row 4 (RS): Holding both cir needle and straight needle in your right hand with cir needle in front of straight needle, *k1 onto cir needle, sl 1 kwise wyf onto straight needle; rep from * to end, pulling knit sts tog firmly, then pm for center of rnd.

Row 5 (RS): Pull right cir needle through sts just worked so you can turn it to work sts from straight needle (similar to Magic Loop), knit all sts from straight needle onto cir needle, pulling sts tog firmly, then pm for beg of rnd. You are now ready to beg working in the rnd.

Flexible Bind-off: K1, *k1, return 2 sts to left needle, k2tog; rep from * to end. Break yarn, leaving a tail, insert tail through last st, and pull to secure.

Instructions

With MC, cir needle, and using the long-tail method, CO 50 sts. Work the "Magic Circle" Start (see Stitch Guide)—100 sts.

Next rnd: *M1, knit to m, M1, sl m; rep from * once more—4 sts inc'd.

Next rnd: Knit.

Rep last 2 rnds 8 more times—136 sts. If you look at your bag end-on now, it will flare like the prow of a Viking ship!

Knit 1 rnd.

Work Rnds 1–160 of color chart.

Knit 6 rnds with MC.

Next rnd: *K5, k2tog; rep from * to last 3 sts, k3—117 sts rem.

Using the Flexible method (see Stitch Guide), BO all sts.

Finishing

Weave in ends. Wash by hand or machine-wash warm on gentle cycle.

Sew on purchased or handwoven strap: Strap is sewn to inside of bag using a sewing machine, but, to keep machine sts invisible on outside, sew between two columns of knit sts. To do this neatly:

Measure strap and decide how many stitch-columns wide it is. For example, mine was 6 stitch-columns wide. Find center of each end of bag, then count half the width of strap in knit columns to each side of center and put a pin to mark outer edge of last column. (So, I counted 3 columns on either side of center and marked the outside of the 3rd column.)

On each side, where marked with pins, use contrasting embroidery thread or other shiny slippery yarn to make loose, long running sts from top to bottom of bag down gap between columns that were marked with pins. This shows on inside of bag, giving a guideline for pinning in strap.

Turn bag inside out and pin one end of strap to inside of bag, centering it all the way across bottom of bag then up one side, using embroidery thread as a guide to center it. (Centering on bottom is pretty easy because of CO seam.)

Sew strap in place from outside, stretching apart columns of knit sts as you go so that sewing lies between them and is hidden. Sts can't be hidden across bottom of bag, but if sewing thread is a good match for MC, they won't show.

Pin other end of strap as for first, overlapping with first across bottom of bag, and making sure strap isn't twisted. (If you make a handwoven strap and overlapping all the way makes the over-the-shoulder part too short, make it fit your shoulder and just overlap at the bottom as far as it will go.) Sew the second side as before, stretching knit columns down the side to hide seam.

Remove embroidery thread and trim any loose ends of sewing thread.

Figure 1. Knitting Color Chart

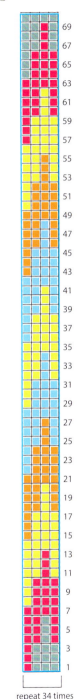

MC
CC1
CC2
CC3
CC4
knit

repeat 34 times

A FLETTED BRAID FOR BAGS AND MORE

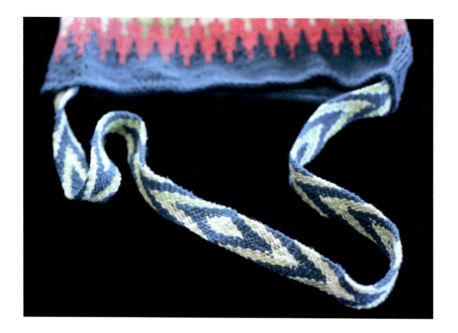

The strap for my market bag is a flat braid, a technique that Scandinavians would call *fletting*. This kind of flat braiding, or finger weaving, has been practiced in many Indigenous cultures around the world, including the Sámi of Scandinavia, Native American communities, and Andean peoples in South America. It's fun and portable, a perfect craft for people who migrate or herd, whether you're taking reindeer or sheep to new pastures or herding the family through a busy week.

This project is written to make a braid for the market bag. The technique is simple, but the braid is long and will take a little patience. If you'd rather just play with fletting, make a shorter warp and weave braid for a bookmark, key fob, or whatever. Choose your own colors, change directions, experiment, go wild!

Structure: Flat braid

Equipment

Three ¼" dowels about 9" long; knitting stitch holder; hair pick with wide teeth; clothes hanging peg that hooks over a door (optional).

Materials

Yarns

Lily Sugar 'n Cream (100% cotton; 190 yd [174 m] per 4 oz "Super Size" ball): Teal and Key Lime Pie Ombre, 48 yd each. (If you knitted the market bag, you should have enough left over for this strap.)

Warp Length

24 ends 4 yd (144") long.

Dimensions

Finished size: One strap, about 1⅛" wide by 82" long.

Notes

- For the dowels, I like to use two pairs of the break-apart wooden chopsticks you get with takeout Chinese food. I break apart one pair and leave the other pair joined at the top. The advantage is that they stay in the warp very well when you set the work down.
- The clothes hook is handy to use as a fixed point to tie your warp on to tension it. You can use a doorknob or table leg, but the hook allows you create a fixed point almost anywhere by hooking it over a door, a chair back, the opposite side of a table, etc.
- For simplicity, I have chosen to call the yarns in this project "the warp." Technically, braiding has no warp or weft; all the yarns simply interlace with each other in different ways at different times, as you will see.
- The dowels used to hold the warp are called "headsticks."
- For the set-up, some finger-weaving instructions will say to put the yarns on the dowel with a clove hitch, and you are welcome to do so. I find a lark's head knot quicker and easier to make, and it doesn't matter which you use because either one will disappear when you pull out the dowel before doing the second half of the braid.
- Because the warp is long, tangles and twists will build up in the unworked yarn as you braid, and you will have to untangle it every so often. Treat it as you would your hair when it's tangled: use the hair pick and/or your fingers to gently comb out the ends, working farther and farther in. Never pull on the twists: just shake gently to loosen them. It's a slow process, but not unpleasant, and the good news is that the Sugar n' Cream yarn holds up to it just fine.
- Whenever you have to stop braiding and put the work down, pick one more shed, slip the knitting stitch holder into it, close the stitch holder, then tie an overhand knot in the loose threads below it. That will help keep the threads organized until you're ready to braid again.

Instructions

Set-up:

1. Wind a warp 4 yd long as follows: 6 ends Teal, 12 ends Key Lime, 6 ends Teal. (You can use a warping board or just wind around the backs of two chairs.) Tie a piece of string tightly about 6" from each end of the warp while still under tension, then cut the loop on the end where you started and ended the winding.

2. Hold the loop end of the warp bundle over your left hand, letting the cut end hang down. With the other hand, pick up one thread at a time by the top of the loop (which is the middle of the thread), make a lark's head knot, and push the knot onto the single dowel. (See photo **1**.) When you finish, center the loops on the dowel. You should have 6 Teal, 12 Key Lime, and 6 Teal knots.

3. Lift the left-hand end hanging from each knot, gather them together, pull them gently up above the dowel, tie together loosely with an overhand knot at the end, and attach that end to the clothes hook or whatever you're using for tensioning.

4. Use another dowel to pick up every other thread of the ones hanging down from the larks head knots, starting from the right and going under-over, then snug it up against the first dowel. Use the third dowel to pick up the opposite threads and snug it up against the second dowel. (If you use a joined chopstick, you'll have to do these two picks at the same time. It's slower, but not difficult.) Your headsticks are now in place, and you're ready to begin braiding. (See photo **2**.)

Braiding:

1. Before you begin the braiding, make sure the opposite end of the warp is attached to a fixed point for tensioning. Sit in a comfortable chair, holding the braiding at a comfortable height to see and work.

1. Put loops on dowel with a lark's head knot.

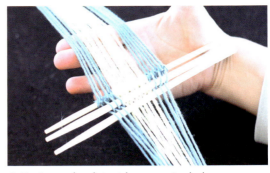

2. Use 2 more dowels to pick up opposite sheds.

3. Pick up opposite shed from the third dowel.

4. Pass thread to the left of center through shed to the right.

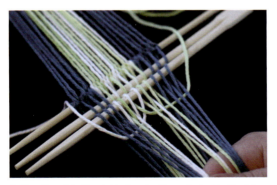

5. Pass thread to the right of center through shed to the left.

6. Pick up next shed and pass left center thread to right as before.

7. As you braid, the chevron pattern will appear.

8. Braiding in the opposite direction forms a diamond in the center of the braid.

2. With the index finger of your left hand, pick up every other thread in the opposite shed from the last headstick and hold them. (See photo **3**.)

3. With your right hand, pick up the Key Lime thread to the left of the center (the 7th one from the right, which will be in the top layer) and pass it all the way to the right through the shed made by your left index finger and lay it on the headsticks to keep it out of the way. (See photo **4**.) Transfer the shed to your right hand. Then pick up the Key Lime thread to the right of center (which will be in the bottom layer, under the thread you just moved to the right) and pass it all the way to the left through the shed made by your finger and lay it to the left on the headsticks, out of the way. (See photo **5**.)

4. Pick up the opposite shed with your right index finger and then transfer it to your left. You can see how to pick up the shed by looking at which threads go over and under the threads you just passed and picking up the threads that went under. Pull the threads you just passed through the shed tight to begin to pull the braid together, then press up into this new shed with your left index finger to snug in the previous pick. (Some diagrams will show the passed threads coming across exactly horizontally, but you can't weave this yarn tight enough to hold them perfectly flat.)

5. In this shed, again pick up the Key Lime thread to the left of the center, pass it all the way to the right through the shed made by your left index finger and lay it on the headsticks to keep it out of the way, then bring the right thread from the previous pick down in front of it to again become part of the "warp" (vertical) threads. (See photo **6**.) Next, pick up the Key Lime thread to the right of center (under the thread you just moved to the right) and pass it all the way to the left through the shed, lay it on the headsticks, then bring the thread from the previous pick down behind it to again become part of the warp threads.

6. Continue in this way, picking sheds and passing the threads to the left and then right of center to the right and left, respectively. As you weave, pull the passed threads from the previous pick tight, being careful to keep the braid a consistent width. When you weave a new pick, always look for the little "X" in the center of the braid that shows you picked the correct middle threads. Braid until you run out of yarn or this side of the braid reaches about 42". As you work, the edge stripes will migrate to the center and the center to the outside, over and over, forming a chevron pattern. (See photo **7**.) Stop and work out twist in the unbraided yarn as needed. (Refer to Notes.)

7. When the first side is finished, tie the leftover ends in an overhand knot, turn the warp around, and attach the end of the braided side to your fixed point. Slip the headsticks out of the unbraided side, catching the upper shed (closest to the braiding) with your left index finger. Carefully pull the threads to tighten the braid, and begin braiding as before, starting with step 3, above. You won't have a headstick to lay the ends on anymore, so I like to slip the double chopstick onto the braid just above where I'm working and lay the ends on it. As you work the first 12 picks, you'll see a diamond form at the center of the braid, and after that there will be chevrons as before. (See photo **8**.)

8. Continue braiding as usual until the second side is the same length and number of repeats as the first. Tie the leftover ends in an overhand knot.

9. When you are ready to use the braid, you can machine sew across the ends with a coordinating thread to stabilize them.

CUP COZIES TO GO

by SARAH SHIPPEN

CRAFT: *Knitting*

DIFFICULTY LEVEL: *Intermediate*

Many local coffee shops in America will serve you in ceramic cups or mugs if you're dining in, as Nordic people do when they meet their friends for *kaffen*. But franchise takeout coffee has penetrated even to fika-focused Scandinavia, although you won't find the famous green mermaid on every corner there. (As of January 2022, Finland had two Starbucks locations for the whole country, and Norway and Sweden had fifteen each at last count.) Sometimes we just need our coffee to go, and if we can't sit down with a real mug, at least we can minimize what we throw away.

Why not buy a reusable to-go cup at your local coffee store and or the housewares section of your grocery, then instead of a paper cuff, dress it up in a miniature Scandinavian sweater? The geometric pattern is based on a woven krokbragd coverlet in the Vesterheim Museum collection, and the flower is based on a traditional pattern from Selbu, Norway.

Structure: Stranded knitting and intarsia

Materials
Yarn Rauma 3-tråds Strikkegarn (100% wool; distributed by The Yarn Guys: 118 yd [108 m] / 1.75 oz [50 g]:

> **MC:** #116 Dark Brown Heather, 1 ball
>
> **CC1:** #460 Light Beige, 1 ball
>
> **CC2:** #124 Red, 1 ball
>
> **CC3:** #177 Dark Orange, 1 ball

Needles Size 4 (3.5 mm): 16"–24" circular (cir) and set of double-pointed (dpn) or additional 16"–24" cir. Adjust needle size if necessary to obtain the correct gauge.

Notions Markers (m); tapestry needle; sewing needle to secure steek stitches.

Gauge 22 sts and 26 rnds = 4" in stranded patt.

Dimensions
Finished Size: 4¼" tall by 9½" circumference top and 8" circumference bottom.

Notes

- The cup cozies are worked in the round from the bottom up.
- The krokbragd pattern is worked in a combination of the stranded knitting and intarsia techniques. To minimize tangles, use a 14" length of yarn for each intarsia color spot. Do not carry color-spot yarns around the row; zig-zag the yarn across the back behind the three-stitch pattern.

Stitch Guide

Alternating-color cable cast-on (ACCO): With MC, place a lark's head knot on left needle with bar at back and tail on left. (See instructions with photos in "The Art of Kaffe: Cozies for a Festive Fika," page 71.)

Insert right needle between legs of knot and wrap CC1 as if to knit. Pull CC1 through, then transfer this st onto left needle as if to knit.

*Insert right needle between last 2 sts on left needle. Pick up MC from behind, pulling it forward, then wrap it around right needle as if to knit, pull new st through, and transfer st to left needle as if to knit.

Bring CC1 from the left and in front of MC, insert right needle between last 2 sts on left needle, wrap CC1 as if to knit, pull new st through, and transfer st to left needle as if to knit.

Rep from * until there is 1 more st on needle than needed. Working yarns will twist as you proceed, so periodically suspend your work by holding both yarns and letting them untwist. Before joining work in the rnd, drop first MC st (left leg of lark's head knot).

Instructions

With cir needle and using the Alternating-Color Cable method (see Stitch Guide), CO 44 sts, ending with CC1. Break CC1.

Knit 2 rows (back and forth) with MC.

Working in St st, work Row 1 of Selbu Flower chart or Krokbragd Flower chart.

Transfer sts to dpn or transfer half to an additional cir needle, pm, and join in the rnd.

Work Rnds 2–26 of chart—52 sts.

BO all sts, alternating MC and CC1 as established on last rnd of chart, making sure that BO is loose enough to maintain gauge of last rnd.

Finishing

Sew CO ends tog. Weave in ends.

Handwash in warm water with mild soap, squeezing and agitating to produce some fulling. Rinse, roll in towel to remove excess moisture, block on a 12 oz to-go coffee cup, and set aside to dry.

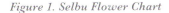

Figure 1. Selbu Flower Chart

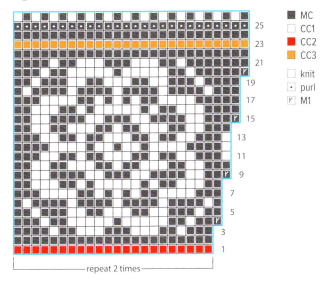

Figure 2. Krokbragd Flower Chart

RYA TO KEEP YOUR PINS COZY

by ANITA OSTERHAUG

CRAFT: *Weaving*

DIFFICULTY LEVEL: *Beginner*

I first learned about rya, the Scandinavian pile weave, by making rya kits with my mother and aunt back in the 1970s. These weren't woven rya: the pile knots were made with a needle, working on a prewoven mesh fabric. When I went to Scandinavia, I fell in love with real, woven rya, especially the bright, nature-inspired designs in Finland.

Rya was invented for blankets used in fishing boats on the west coast of Norway, where the traditional sheepskin blankets would be damaged by salt water. The technique goes back to at least the seventeenth century, but it was in the early twentieth century that rya rugs, pillows, and wall hangings became a popular part of interior design.

Once I learned to do woven rya, I realized that it could also be a great way to use up small amounts of yarn left from other weaving projects. This project was inspired by a pillow my grandmother brought from Norway. It has a pattern in rya knots but is unusual in that the knots are made of a bulky yarn, and they are closely cropped to make the pile design stand out on a plain-weave ground. I had a nice stash of leftover Norwegian yarn from other projects—yarn that would be more typical for rya—so I decided to try weaving a miniature pillow, a pincushion, to practice my rya skills while avoiding waste. The project directions are written so you can make two pincushions, one for you and one for a friend.

Structure: Plain weave with rya knots

Equipment
Rigid-heddle loom, 10" weaving width; 12-dent reed; 1 stick shuttle; small pick-up stick.

Materials
Yarns

Warp: 12/6 cotton (1,450 yd/lb; Bockens), #4467 natural, 148 yd.

Weft: 2-ply wool tapestry yarn (100% Spelsau wool; 330 yd/100 gm; 1,500 yd/lb; Rauma Prydvev yarn (Blue Heron), #601, white.

Rya knots: (used doubled; includes amounts for decorative braid): 2-ply wool tapestry yarn, #681 (red brown), 52 yd; #690 (olive), 32 yd; #658 (light green), 28 yd; #619 (gold), 36 yd.

Other supplies: Fray Check; polyester fill or batting.

Warp Length

84 ends 1¾ yd long (allows 3" for take-up, 28" for knotting practice and loom waste).

Setts

Warp: 12 epi.

Weft: About 22 ppi.

Dimensions
Width in the reed: 7" in a 10-dent reed.

Woven length: (measured under tension on the loom) 32".

Finished size: Two pincushions, 5½" by 7".

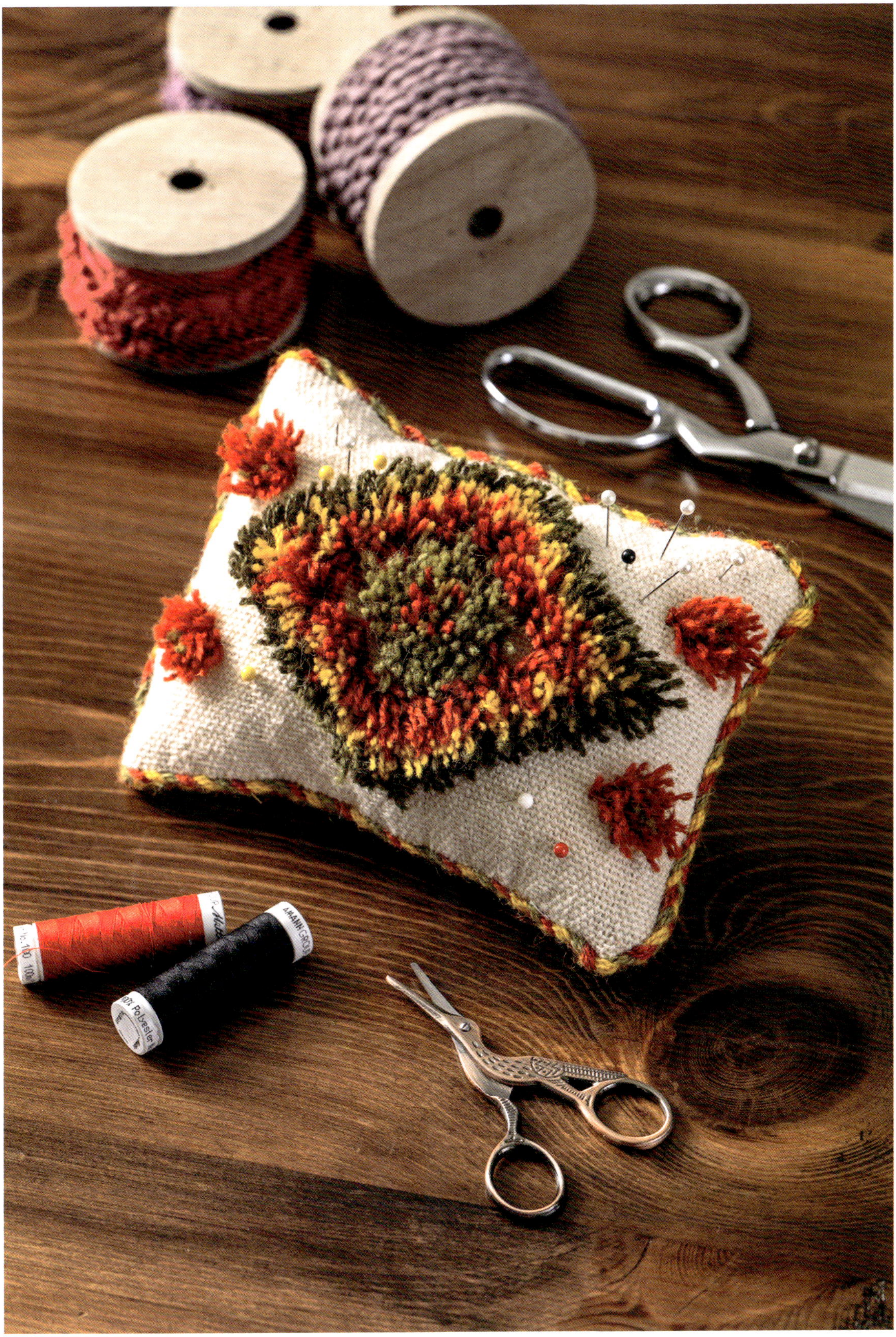

Grandma Osterhaug's unusual rya pillow

Instructions

1. Wind 84 warp ends 1³/₄ yd long. Warp the loom for plain weave using your preferred method, centering for 7".

2. Wind a bobbin with the white wool weft.

Figure 1. Rya Knotting Chart

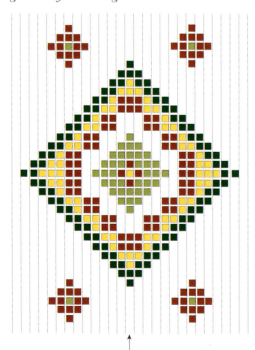

3. Spread the warp with waste yarn. Weave 9" in plain weave, then begin weaving the rows of rya knots, following the chart in figure 1 and weaving 4 weft picks between each row of knots. (See inset for rya knot instructions.) Once you complete the rya design, weave another 1" in plain weave, then cut the pile to your desired length. I left mine about ¹/₄", but you could cut yours shorter if you want the design to be more crisp. After trimming the pile, weave 2 picks of contrasting scrap yarn, then weave another pincushion as you did the first.

4. Put Fray Check along both ends of the fabric and on either side of the scrap yarn and allow to dry. Remove the fabric from the loom and cut the pincushions apart at the scrap yarn.

5. To assemble each pincushion, fold in half, right sides together, and sew a seam ¹/₂" from the fold. Pin sides carefully and sew side seams ³/₈" from selvedges. Turn pincushion right side out and fill with stuffing, using a chopstick or knitting needle to push the stuffing into the corners. (If you use polyester batting, you can fold it to the right size and insert, but make sure it pushes clear into the corners.) After stuffing, fold open ends inside the pincushion and sew closed by hand using a blind stitch, leaving one corner open about ¹/₄".

6. For the braid: Measure out three 2-yd lengths each of red brown, gold, and the light green yarn. Line up the yarns of each color, lay the color groups side by side, and knot one end of the whole yarn bundle. Anchor the knotted end in whatever way is convenient (I tucked the knot into a closed drawer), then braid a 3-strand braid, weaving each color group as one strand. Tuck the knot into the open spot on the pincushion, then sew braid over the pincushion seams, alternately catching the back of the braid and the threads on either side of the seam. When you come back to the open spot, cut the remaining braid to 1", knot the end, tuck end inside the pincushion, and sew the open spot shut.

Weaving Rya Knots

For each knot color, measure out 1 yd of yarn at a time and fold in half.

Each rya knot covers 2 warp ends. To make a knot, identify the two warp ends you will cover. If you are doing a row of knots in the same color, start at the right-most warp ends for that row. Coming from the right, tuck about ½" of the loose ends of the knot yarn under the right warp end. (See photo **1**.) Bring the long end of the warp to the left going over both warp ends, tuck the folded end under the left warp end and bring it up to center below where the yarn crosses (See photo **2**.), then pull the knot tight. (See photo **3**.) If you will be making an adjacent knot in the same color, leave a ½" tall loop of yarn as you begin the next knot. If this is the last knot of this color, cut the working yarn, leaving ½" tail.

You can do all the knots of one color in a row and then fill in the other colors. Just count your warp threads carefully to make sure you don't skip one between knots or accidentally cover more than 2.

I wove 4 weft picks between each row of knots, which made a long diamond. If you want your design to be more square, you could weave 2 or 3 picks between knot rows. Your warp length includes enough length for some sampling. If you make your diamond shorter, you can either let the pincushion be shorter or weave more plain weave at either end of the design.

Before trimming your rya pile, go back and cut all the loops. Having all open ends will allow you to cut the pile to a more consistent height. I recommend trimming one row of knots at a time, separating the rows with your fingers and measuring each row against the one before it.

Trimming creates a lot of lint, so gently brush, blow, or vacuum off the lint after trimming.

1. Tuck yarn end under right warp end.

2. Bring yarn around and under left warp end.

3. Pull rya knot tight.

Back of fabric showing the knots.

WHERE TO GO FROM HERE

I hope you've enjoyed this smörgåsbord of Nordic history, culture, and folk and fiber arts. Like any other Nordic buffet, it was created so that you could browse, enjoy, and take away what appeals to you. To me, a Nordic life is one of curiosity, the pleasure of creating for oneself, and being grounded in nature, community, and sustainability. I wish you those things.

If you have an appetite for more, there are many resources available and paths to explore. I've listed my favorite Nordic museums and fiber arts schools in the "Resources" section, as well as suppliers of yarn and books. Many of the artisans who contributed projects to this book are also excellent teachers whom I know you would enjoy. And the bibliography lists lots of books and some online resources, in case you want to dig deeper into any of the techniques in this book or other Nordic fiber arts such as *nålbinding* (knotless netting) or *sprang*, another very old and traditional Scandinavian textile technique.

Wherever your curiosity and hands take you, may you have safe travels and grand adventures.

Sprang bag by Carol James

Alta Mile Post, Alta, Norway. Photo by John Capone.

1. T. K. Derry, *A History of Scandinavia* (Minneapolis: University of Minnesota Press, 1979), 5–10.
2. Ibid.
3. According to the historian T. K. Derry, the prayer also included pleas to be spared gratuitous throat cutting and other horrors at the hands of the invading Norsemen.
4. Derry, *A History of Scandinavia*, 190.
5. Mart Kuldkepp, "Emigration and Scandinavian Identity," in *Introduction to Nordic Cultures*, ed. Annika Lindskog and Jakob Stougaard-Nielsen (London: UCL, 2020), 181–94.
6. "Trend Watch: How to Create Japandi Style." www.boconcept.com/en-us/inspiration/trends/japandi-style.
7. "Social Environments for World Happiness." www.worldhappiness.report/ed/2020/social-environments-for-world-happiness.
8. "World Happiness Index." www.countryeconomy.com/demography/world-happiness-index.
9. Jukka Savolainen, "The Grim Secret of Nordic Happiness," *Slate*, April 28, 2021, www.slate.com/news-and-politics/2021/04/finland-happiness-lagom-hygge.html.
10. Michael Booth, *The Almost Nearly Perfect People: Behind the Myth of the Scandinavian Utopia* (New York: Picador, 2016).
11. Jen Rose Smith, "What Is 'Friluftsliv'? How an Idea of Outdoor Living Could Help Us This Winter," *National Geographic*, September 2020, www.nationalgeographic.com/travel/article/how-norways-friluftsliv-could-help-us-through-a-coronavirus-winter.
12. Andrea Immel, "If It's Christmas, It's Time for Swedish Dala Horses, Part 1," www.blogs.princeton.edu/cotsen/2020/12/if-its-christmas-its-time-for-swedish-dala-horses-part-i/.
13. "Expat Insider 2017: Looking at the World through Expat Eyes," www.cms-internationsgmbh.netdna-ssl.com/cdn/file/2017-09/Expat_Insider_2017_The_InterNations_Survey.pdf.
14. It should also be noted, however, that Norway, Sweden, and Denmark ranked high for peacefulness, quality of life, and being desirable countries in which to settle.
15. Aksel Sandemose, *A Fugitive Crosses His Tracks (En Flyktning Krysser Sitt Spor)* (New York: A. A. Knopf, 1936; first published in 1933).
16. *Janteloven* in Danish and Norwegian, *Jantelagen* in Swedish, *Jante laki* in Finnish, and *Jantelögin* in Icelandic.
17. Brontë Aurell, *Scandikitchen Fika & Hygge* (New York: Ryland Peters and Small, 2016), 30–31.
18. Booth, *The Almost Nearly Perfect People*, 154.
19. Travel + Leisure, www.travelandleisure.com/culture-design/kalsarikannit-new-hygge.
20. Hasvold, Carol. "Ale Bowls and Festive Events in Traditional Norway." *Vesterheim* 6, no. 1 (2008).
21. Katherine Larson, *The Woven Coverlets of Norway* (Seattle: University of Washington Press, 2001).
22. Mary B. Kelly, *Embroidering the Goddesses of Old Norway* (Hilton Head, SC: Studiobooks, 2008).
23. Janice Stewart, *The Folk Arts of Norway* (Rhinelander, WI: Nordhus, 1999).
24. Ibid., 46.

NOTES

25. Clasped-weft means that when two weft colors in a tapestry turn around adjacent warp threads, they are clasped around each other so that there is no gap or slit in the fabric. A kilim rug is an example of the opposite technique, where adjacent color areas will have a slit between them.

26. Gilbertson, Laurann, and Kathleen Stokker, "Weaving Bewitchment: Gerhard Munthe's Folk-Tale Tapestries," *Norwegian Textile Newsletter* 1, no. 2 (2003).

27. Åse Enerstvedt, *Ragna Beivik: Et liv ved veven* (Østerås, Norway: Edie Forlag, 1991).

28. Sonja Berlin, *Tablet-Weaving—in True Nordic Fashion* (Malmköping, Sweden: Brickvävnad [Sonja Berlin]), 2017), 13–35.

29. Stewart, *The Folk Arts of Norway*, 176–78.

30. Susan Foulkes, *Weaving Patterned Bands: How to Create and Design with 5, 7, and 9 Pattern Threads* (Atglen, PA: Schiffer, 2018), 17–18.

31. Ibid., 16.

32. Susanne Pagoldh, *Nordic Knitting: Thirty-One Patterns in the Scandinavian Tradition* (Loveland, CO: Interweave, 1991), 11.

33. Derry, *A History of Scandinavia*, 142.

34. Stewart, *The Folk Arts of Norway*, 123–24.

35. Rikard Berge, *Norskt Bondesylv* (Risør, Norway: Erik Gunleikson, 1925), 14.

36. Berlin, *Tablet-Weaving*, 66–67.

37. Lila Nelson, "The Ruteaklear Tradition in Norway," *Norwegian Textile Newsletter* 1, no. 2 (January 1995).

38. "Will Ferrell Super Bowl Ad—General Motors," www.youtube.com/watch?v=mdsPvbSpB2Y. (Fun fact: Ferrell's wife, actor Viveca Paulin, is Swedish. For more fun, search YouTube for "Norway's Answer to Will Ferrell."

39. Robin Taylor, ed. (*Oak—the Nordic Journal*), *The Red Thread: Nordic Design* (New York: Phaidon, 2017), 9.

40. Stewart, *The Folk Arts of Norway*, 34.

41. "A World of Vernacular Furniture: The Kubbestol/Kubbstol," www.smow.com/blog/2021/01/a-world-of-vernacular-furniture the-kubbestol-kubbstol/.

42. David Palm, Maria Elander, David Watson, et al., "A Nordic Textile Strategy, Part II: A Proposal for Increased Collection, Sorting, Reuse and Recycling of Textiles," Nordic Council of Ministers, 2014, www.norden.diva-portal.org/smash/get/diva2:791003/fulltext01.pdf.

ACBO alternating color bind-off: On row before bind-off by k all sts, alternating MC and CC, then BO, alternating colors as in previous row.

ACCO alternating color cable cast on (instructions given in projects)

beg begin(ning)

BLCO backward loop cast-on: Make a slipknot about 3" from end of yarn and place on needle. Holding needle in right hand, bring yarn from needle behind tip of left index finger, rotate finger to your right to make a loop around finger. With needle, pick up loop on finger from below, then tighten on needle. Repeat for desired numbers of stitches.

BO bind off

CC contrasting color

brk brioche knit

brp brioche purl

ch chain

cir circular needle

cn cable needle

CO cast on

cont continu(e)(ing)

dec decrease(ed)

dpn double-pointed needle(s)

foll follows

k knit

k1f&b knit through the front and back of the same stitch

k1tbl knit 1 through back loop

k2tog knit 2 together

kwise knitwise; as if to knit

LTCO long-tail cast-on

m marker

M1 insert left needle under running thread between stitches from front to back and knit this stitch through the back loop

M1P insert left needle under running thread between stitches from front to back and purl this stitch through the back loop

MC main color

p purl

p2tog purl 2 together

p5tog purl 5 together

p7tog purl 7 together

patt pattern

pm place marker

psso pass slipped stitch over

pwise purlwise; as if to purl

rem remain(s)

rep repeat

rnd(s) round(s)

RS right side

sl slip

slp slip as if to purl

slyo slip 1 yarnover

ssk [sl 1 kwise] 2 times, insert left needle into front of these 2 sts and work them tog

ssp [sl 1 kwise] 2 times, return 2 sts to left needle, p2tog tbl

st(s) stitch(es)

tbl through back loop

tog together

WS wrong side

wyb with yarn in back

wyf with yarn in front

yo yarnover

ytb yarn to back of work

ytf yarn to front of work

* starting point of repeat

[ ] work instructions as a group the specified number of times

WEAVING GLOSSARY

back beam: Bar at the back of the loom that holds the unwoven warp.

beaming: Winding the warp on the back beam of the loom.

beat: To press a weft pick into place.

closed shed: When no shed is open and all warp threads are at the same height.

cloth beam: The wooden beam at the front of the loom where cloth builds up as a warp is woven.

direct warping: A method of warping rigid-heddle looms where the warp is strung out between a warping peg and the apron rod of the loom instead of being measured on a warping board.

draw-in: Narrowing of weaving at the selvedge due to the weft going over and under the warp yarn. All weaving has some draw-in. Excessive draw-in can happen when weft picks are placed in too tight.

ends per inch (epi): The number of warp ends in one inch of weaving (also called *sett*).

ends: One or more warp threads that always weave together. Usually one thread, but sometimes a yarn is used doubled or tripled.

fell: The edge of the weaving where the last weft has been beaten into place.

float: Any place where a warp thread goes over more than one weft thread (warp float) or a weft thread goes over more than one warp thread (weft float).

fulling: The partial felting of wool during wet-finishing to stabilize and relax the threads in woven cloth.

header: First inch or so of weaving that helps the warp threads spread out evenly.

leno: A technique where warp ends are crossed over each other, usually by hand, to create lacy openings.

loom waste: Length of warp that cannot be woven when weaving nears the end of the warp.

open shed: When some warp ends are lifted or lowered to create an opening, the shed is open.

picks per inch (ppi): The number of weft picks in 1" of weaving.

pick: One pass of the weft through a shed.

pick-up stick: A flat wooden stick used to manipulate warp threads.

plain weave: The simplest weave structure, where each pick of weft goes over one warp thread, then under the next, and the picks alternate which threads they go over and under.

rigid-heddle loom: A loom where sheds are made by raising or lowering a rigid heddle, a solid plastic comb with alternating holes and slots.

selvedges: The right and left edges of your woven cloth. Sometimes also refers to the final warp end on either side.

sett: The number of warp ends per inch (epi).

shed: The opening created when the shafts are lifted. Weft picks go through sheds.

shot: Alternate term for *pick*.

shrinkage: The percentage of size decrease when cloth is wet-finished.

shuttle: A tool for carrying weft through the shed. Stick shuttles carry weft wound onto the stick.

take-up: The amount of warp length used up by warp ends traveling over and under the weft picks.

tension: How tightly warp threads are held by the loom.

threading: The process of putting warp threads through the heddle.

warp: The threads held under tension on the loom.

warping board: Frame with pegs used to measure out warp. The warp is made by winding back and forth between pegs.

weft: The threads that weave between the warp threads. They are perpendicular to the selvedge and run horizontally on the cloth.

wet-finishing: Washing finished weaving to help the warp and weft relax and bind together (see *fulling*).

NORDIC ORGANIZATIONS

American Swedish Institute
2600 Park Avenue, Minneapolis, MN 55407
asimn.org

Canadian Nordic Society
240 Sparks Street
PO Box 55023
Ottawa, ON
Canada K1P 1A1
canadiannordicsociety.com

Canadian Scandinavian Foundation
1438 Rue Fullum
Montreal, QC
Canada H2K 3M1
thecsfoundation.com

Finnish Heritage Museum
301 High Street
Fairport Harbor, OH 44077
finnishheritagemuseum.org

Finlandia Foundation
finlandiafoundation.org

Museum of Danish America
2212 Washington Street
Elk Horn, IA 51531
danishmuseum.org

National Nordic Museum
2655 NW Market Street
Seattle, WA 98107
nordicmuseum.org

Swedish-American Museum
5211 N. Clark Street
Chicago, IL 60640
swedishamericanmuseum.org

Vesterheim National Norwegian-American Museum
520 W. Water Street
Decorah, IA 52101
vesterheim.org

NORDIC FIBER ARTS INSTRUCTION

Nordic Knitting Conference
National Nordic Museum
2655 NW Market Street
Seattle, WA 98107
nordicmuseum.org

Norwegian Textile Newsletter
(history and techniques)
1801 Fremont Avenue South, #2
Minneapolis, MN 55403
norwegiantextileletter.com

Red Stone Glen (weaving)
435 Popps Ford Road
York Haven, PA 17370
redstoneglen.com

Vesterheim Folk Art School
(weaving and other fiber arts)
520 W. Water Street
Decorah, IA 52101
vesterheim.org

Vävstuga Weaving School
80 Bassett Road
Shelburne, MA 01370
www.vavstuga.com

SUPPLIERS

Blue Heron Knittery (Rauma weaving and
knitting yarns, knitting needles and notions,
books)
300 W. Water Street
Decorah, IA 52101
www.blueheronknittery.com

Glimakra USA (weaving equipment, Bockens and
other Scandinavian yarns, books)
2750 Roosevelt Blvd Unit G
Eugene, OR 97402
www.glimakrausa.com/home

Halcyon Yarn (Lopi yarn, knitting and weaving
equipment, books)
12 School Street
Bath, ME 04530
www.halcyonyarn.com

Nordic Yarn Imports, Ltd.
#301 - 5327 192nd Street
Surrey, BC
Canada V3S 8E5
www.nordicyarnimports.com/retailers.htm (list of
retailers in Canada)

North Star Homestead (needlefelting and tapestry
supplies)
11077 N. Fullington Road
Hayward, WI 54843
www.northstarhomestead.com

Red Stone Glen (weaving equipment, yarn, books)
435 Popps Ford Rd
York Haven, PA 17370
www.redstoneglen.com

StoorStålka (band-weaving equipment and yarns)
Föreningsgatan 2
96232 Jokkmokk
Sweden
www.bandweaving.com

The Yarn Guys (North American Rauma yarn
distributor)
8 W Stephenson Street
Freeport, IL 61032
www.theyarnguys.com

Vävstuga Weaving School (weaving equipment,
Bockens and other Scandinavian yarns,
books)
80 Bassett Road
Shelburne, MA 01370
www.vavstuga.com

Yarn Canada
30-333 28 Street NE
Calgary, AB
Canada T2A 7P4
www.yarncanada.ca

Aurell, Brönte. *Scandikitchen Fika & Hygge*. New York: Ryland Peters & Small, 2016.

Berlin, Sonja. *Tablet-Weaving—in True Nordic Fashion*. Malmköping, Sweden: Brickvävnad (Sonja Berlin), 2017.

Booth, Michael. *The Almost Nearly Perfect People: Behind the Myth of the Scandinavian Utopia*. New York: Picador, 2016.

Derry, T. K. *A History of Scandinavia*. Minneapolis: University of Minnesota Press, 1979.

Edenheim, Ralph, and Eivor Martinus, eds. *Skansen: Traditional Swedish Style*. Translated by Neil Smith. London: Scala, 1995.

Enerstvedt, Åse. *Ragna Beivik: Et liv ved veven*. Østerås, Norway: Edie Forlag, 1991.

Englund, Sonja Berlin. *Brickvävning—så in i Norden*. Kalmar, Sweden: Brickvävnad, 1994.

Findley, Gerald L. *Fingerweaving Basics*. Hermon, NY: Gerald L. Findley, 2005.

Foulkes, Susan J. 2013, *The Art of Simple Band Weaving*. http://www.blurb.com, 2013.

Gilbertson, Laurann, and Kathleen Stokker. "Weaving Bewitchment: Gerhard Munthe's Folk-Tale Tapestries." *Norwegian Textile Newsletter* 1, no. 2 (2003).

Hasvold, Carol. "Ale Bowls and Festive Events in Traditional Norway." *Vesterheim* 6, no. 1 (2008).

Hennig, Reinhard, Anna-Karin Jonasson, and Peter Degerman, eds. *Nordic Narratives of Nature and the Environment: Ecocritical Approaches to Northern European Literatures and Cultures*. Lanham, MD: Lexington Books, 2018.

Ingstad, Anne Stine. "The Textiles in the Oseberg Ship." http://www.forest.gen.nz/Medieval/articles/Oseberg/textiles/textile.htm.

James, Carol. *Fingerweaving Untangled*. Winnipeg, MB: Carol James, 2011.

James, Carol. *Sprang Unsprung*. Winnipeg, MB: Carol James, 2011.

Johansson, Gunvor. *Heirlooms of Skåne: Weaving Techniques*. Translated by Birgitta Esselius Peterson. Shelburne, MA: Vävstuga, 2016.

Jónasson, Björn. *Hávamál: The Sayings of the Vikings*. Reykjavík, Iceland: Gudrun, 1992.

Kelly, Mary B. *Embroidering the Goddesses of Norway*. Hilton Head, SC: Studiobooks, 2008.

Kinsella, Kasja. *Nordicana: 100 Icons of Scandi Culture and Nordic Cool*. London: Octopus, 2015.

LaFleur, Robbie, ed. *Norwegian Textile Newsletter*. norwegiantextileletter.com.

Larson, Katherine. *The Woven Coverlets of Norway*. Seattle: University of Washington Press, 2001.

Linskog, Annika, and Jakob Sougaard-Nielsen, eds. *Introduction to Nordic Cultures*. London: University College of London, 2020.

Magnusson, Helene. *Icelandic Handknits*. Minneapolis: Voyageur, 2013.

McDonald, Julie Jensen. *Scandinavian Proverbs: Folk Wisdom from Denmark, Finland, Iceland, Norway, and Sweden*. Iowa City, IA: Penfield, 1985.

Mullarkey, John, Marilyn Emerson Holtzer, Luise Hoffman, Jo Ann Treumann, and Bonnie White. *A Tablet Weaver's Pattern Book*. St. Louis, MO: John Mullarkey, 2007.

Nelson, Lila. "The Ruteaklear Tradition in Norway." *Norwegian Textile Newsletter* 1, no. 2 (January 1995).

Pagoldh, Susanne. *Nordic Knitting: Thirty-One Patterns in the Scandinavian Tradition*. Loveland, CO: Interweave, 1991.

Partanen, Anu. *The Nordic Theory of Everything: In Search of a Better Life*. New York: Harper Paperbacks, 2016.

Patrick, Jane. *The Weaver's Idea Book: Creative Cloth on a Rigid Heddle Loom*. Loveland, CO: Interweave, 2010.

Rutt, Richard. *A History of Hand Knitting*. Loveland, CO: Interweave, 1987.

Stewart, Janice. *The Folk Arts of Norway*. Rhinelander, WI: Nordhus, 1999.

Taylor, Robin, ed. (*Oak—the Nordic Journal*), *The Red Thread: Nordic Design*. New York: Phaidon, 2017.

Textile Museum of Canada. *Marimekko, with Love*. Toronto, ON: Textile Museum of Canada, 2013.

Birgit Albiker-Osterhaug

From her early years, Birgit experienced *handarbeiten* (handwork) as part of daily life, as her mother sewed many of their clothes and knitted sweaters for Birgit and her four brothers. Both her parents were skilled in crafts, which meant that the family spent many evenings making ornaments, mosaics, jewelry, or fiber arts projects. German schools still include fiber arts in their weekly curriculum and today expose both genders to knitting, crocheting, and related skills. Birgit became a serious knitter in her teen years, when she discovered modern designs and newly created fashion yarns. Today, she focuses on lace knitting as a particular challenge. She has designed many garments and accessories for friends and family over the years, and this is her debut as a professional designer. She says, "It has been challenging to discover the trial and error of fitting stitches to images but has also proven fascinating and enjoyable to realize that I am able not only to execute others' ideas, but to develop and bring to life my own."

Becky Ashenden

Becky's 1981 introduction to the wealth of the Swedish textile world at Sätergläntan Institutet för Slöjd och Hantverk, a school renowned for weaving and other traditional crafts since 1922, gave her the motivation to pursue weaving as a life passion as well as a career. Her use of equipment and techniques that have withstood the test of time adds to the value of what she has been offering her students at Vävstuga Weaving School since 1991. Becky has also worked on a series of publishing projects for her own Vävstuga Press, which includes translating weaving books from Swedish to English and republishing Swedish weaving books that have gone out of print. Becky is also a professional musician in a variety of folk music traditions from Swedish to Balkan to Cape Breton, playing several instruments including piano, accordion, and fiddle.

Laura Berlage

Laura is a contemporary Renaissance woman living and working on her family's century-old homestead farm outside Hayward, Wisconsin. From fiber arts to creative writing, music to storytelling, she never tires of the magic of transforming idea into form and overlapping narrative and visual. Laura also loves working with the varied and beautiful natural materials from her farm—especially the wool from her sheep. Since completing her MFA in interdisciplinary arts at Goddard College in 2011, Laura has continued her lifelong passion for learning, teaching engaged, hands-on classes for small groups to encourage creativity, imagination, and expression. Currently, her virtual fiber arts instruction collaborates with Nordic-related organizations, including Vesterheim Folk Arts School, the American Swedish Institute, and North House Folk School. You can keep up with Laura at www.erindaletapestrystudio.com.

Sara Bixler

Sara is the owner and resident instructor of Red Stone Glen Fiber Arts Center. She is an expert weaver both on multishaft and rigid-heddle looms. Many of Sara's students praise her ability to guide students through the challenging world of color theory, specifically relating to weaving. Sara has spent many years experimenting with color in weaving, studying how color relationships are affected by yarn size, luster, sett, and weave structure. You can find her weaving videos at www.learn.longthread media.com.

Deb Carpenter-Beck

Deb is a longtime spinner, knitter, and weaver. She is fascinated with the variety of textiles the world over and often uses elements from different cultures as inspiration in her own design work. Most days you will find her in her home studio playing with fiber and fabric.

Susan J. Foulkes

Susan is a designer/weaver in love with natural yarns and fascinated by the long history of weaving. She gained her HNC in art and design (handloom textile design) in 2001. Exploring the many facets of weaving brought her into contact with the woven patterned bands from around the Baltic region, which became the focus for her research. Susan has published several books of band patterns and more than twenty YouTube videos, and she has introduced the use of the double-slotted heddle through workshops in the United Kingdom, the United States, and online. She lives in England, and you can read about her work at www.durhamweaver64.blogspot.com.

Elisabeth Hill

Many years ago, Lisa took a beginning weaving class with Scott Norris at WEBS, finished the class, and bought a loom, and she's been weaving nonstop ever since. (As a child, her now-grown son described her as "a very make-y person.") Lisa completed a six-year Master Weaver Program at Hill Institute in Florence, Massachusetts, in 2012. She is the program chair for the Weavers of Western Massachusetts. She believes that cloth and its creation are somehow embedded in our DNA, and she designs to create items that will be in daily use, but that demonstrate that utility is not "mere utility" but is intimately entwined with our aesthetic needs. She has been a technical editor and frequent contributor to *Handwoven* magazine, and she has taught at Vävstuga Weaving School and at Harrisville Designs.

Carol James

Carol has been playing with strings for a long time; she learned to embroider and to crochet before she entered kindergarten. Since the 1980s she has been exploring the flat braiding technique known in North America as finger weaving. In the mid-1990s, she was introduced to *sprang*. She has spent the past twenty years rediscovering textile forms that had been considered lost, resurrecting these ancient techniques and making them accessible to everyone through her publications, books, and workshops. She is the author of *Fingerweaving Untangled* and *Sprang Unsprung*. You can follow her adventures at www.spranglady.com/blog, and her video series on finger weaving and sprang are available at www.taprootvideo.com. Carol believes that textile creation is part of our human heritage and that woven together we are stronger.

Tom Knisely

Tom has made his career from his interest and love of textiles from around the world. Tom has been studying about, collecting, and teaching others about weaving and spinning for more than four decades, making him one of the most well-versed weaving instructors in North America. In addition to teaching, Tom weaves professionally and is a frequent contributor to *Handwoven* magazine. Voted *Handwoven*'s Teacher of the Year, Tom is renowned among his students for his kindness, good humor, and "seemingly infinite knowledge on the subject of weaving." You can find his weaving videos at www.learn.longthreadmedia.com.

Jan Mostrom

Jan learned to weave at a class at Luther College, and she has never stopped exploring and learning, with a special interest in Scandinavian weaving. She is mostly self-taught but has had generous mentors in Lila Nelson and Syvilla Bolson and has built her skills in a variety of weaving techniques through classes from Norwegian instructors at Vesterheim Norwegian-American Museum and through classes in Scandinavia. Jan has been a member of the Scandinavian Study Group for over twenty-five years, led an international study group on Danskbrogd, and has written articles for the *Norwegian Textile Newsletter*. She has taught classes at Vesterheim Folk Art School and the Weavers Guild of Minnesota and has presented papers at various conferences, including the first Norwegian Textile Conference at Vesterheim.

John Mullarkey

A nationally recognized teacher, John has been tablet weaving for over a decade. His work has been displayed in the Missouri History Museum, and garments using his card-woven bands have been featured in international fashion shows. His designs are featured frequently in *Handwoven* magazine. John is the primary author of *A Tablet Weaver's Pattern Book*, and he has produced two DVDs for *Handwoven*: "Tablet Weaving Made Easy" and "Double-Faced Tablet Weaving." He is also the developer of the Schacht Zoom Loom. You can see what John's been up to at www.malarkycrafts.com, and you can find his weaving videos at www.learn.longthreadmedia.com.

Christiane Payton

Christiane is an artist living in rural western Oregon. She has enjoyed creating as well as working with animals for as long as she can remember. Now that the family's four young adult children have fledged the nest, she spends even more time on her artistic pursuits, which are primarily drawing, watercolor painting, and oil painting. When not in front of an easel, she loves to ride her horse, work in the garden, hike with her husband, Mark, and travel.

Sarah Shippen

Sarah has been knitting, spinning, and weaving for more than thirty years. (In fact, she was the fiber-holic and enabler who lured the author into spinning and then weaving.) She holds a BA from Barnard College in art history and a master of architecture from the University of Illinois. Having recently retired from architecture, she is now pursuing her lifelong love of textiles. She has studied Scandinavian textile traditions at Vesterheim and at Nordic Knitting Conferences at the National Nordic Museum. Sarah brings an artist's sense of shape and color and an architect's eye for detail to her knitting and weaving. She experiments fearlessly, samples relentlessly, and chooses every detail, from cast-on to bind-off and finishing, to make her designs as perfect as they can be. She has been published in *Piecework* magazine.

INDEX

Anita Osterhaug is an editor emerita of *Handwoven* magazine. An author and journalist, she studied history and anthropology at Reed College. Anita is devoted to textiles, and her skills include embroidery, knitting, weaving, spinning, felting, and dyeing. Her focus on Scandinavian textiles is extensive, from childhood knitting and embroidery lessons with her Norwegian aunt and grandmother to programs at Vesterheim Museum, the Norwegian Textile Guild, and the National Nordic Museum, classes in Scandinavia, and her own research.